Why We Are Born

Remembering Our Purpose
through the Akashic Records

Akemi G

Disclaimer

The author is not a healthcare professional and no part of this book is to be regarded as medical advice. This book offers insights and information from the author's personal perspective; in the event the reader uses any of the information in this book for themselves or others, the reader assumes full responsibility for their understanding, actions, and the results.

Love and gratitude
to all,

Contents

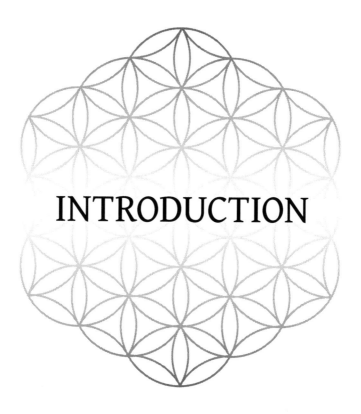

INTRODUCTION

For things to reveal themselves to us,
we need to be ready to abandon
our views about them.
— Thich Nhat Hanh

Our natural search for purpose

"Why am I born?"

"Am I meant to do something in life?"

"What is the purpose of life? What is my purpose?"

These questions pop up in our hearts spontaneously. We already know the biological mechanism of birth—conception and pregnancy. However, something in us knows there is a deeper meaning. It's like trying to remember something important that we learned long ago. We know we knew it. It's just that now, we cannot remember it well. This is frustrating.

As we go through our day-to-day life, we keep wondering, "What is this all about?" We simply cannot accept the idea that life is a meaningless repetition of getting out of bed, doing things, and going back to bed. Surely, there must be a purpose.

Is it just wishful thinking that life has a purpose, or is it real? If it is real, what is that purpose? How do we know? Can we prove it?

We have always been asking these questions. Various philosophers and religious teachers have attempted to answer them, and yet, we keep asking. We are missing something in our quest.

The false model of life

We usually think of life as something like this: We are conceived and born. We don't choose to be born—we are just born. We go to school. We find a job and work to make a living. We grow old.

Someday, for one reason or another, we die. For some of us, this is the end. Some believe we go to heaven or hell. Some believe in reincarnation, which might bring comfort because it means life continues after death. Others may dread the same idea of reincarnation because it means we are stuck in eternal cycles of birth and death.

As long as we view life this way, there is no meaningful answer to the question, "Why are we born?" The premise is inaccurate and insufficient, so it leads to inaccurate and insufficient conclusions.

Our life didn't start at birth and doesn't end at death. One lifetime's birth and death are only parts of the soul's long life. This means we are far more than we usually think we are. It also means we need to understand where we were before birth and where we are going after death. In other words, we need to know what "there" is like to know why we are "here."

Collective wisdom in the Akashic Records

In this book, I'd like to share information and insights that I have had the honor to gather while working in the Hall of the Akashic Records. The Akashic Records are the energetic records of all souls. Everything that has ever happened, is happening, and can happen is recorded in the Akashic Records. The word "Akashic" comes from the Sanskrit word "Akasha," which means the universal, primordial energy. The Akashic Records, however, are not just about the ancient South Asians.

The existence of such energetic records has been known by people worldwide and is called by various other names, including the "Book of Life" in the Bible. Further, the Akashic Records are more than a dry compilation of past, present, and future events. They also contain our collective wisdom that we have gathered through various experiences.

Can we prove the existence of such energetic records and verify the reliability of their wisdom? Not by the current level of science and its approach. The scientific approach is based on things that can be observed and measured. However, the tools we currently have for such observation and measurement are grossly primitive and limited. So we have a dilemma here.

The soul's life expands beyond what we can observe with our current tools. Our inability to gather data doesn't mean things don't exist beyond the perceived limitation. There are many truths that are yet to be proved simply because we are not appropriately equipped at this time.

This means we have to set aside our existing knowledge about life in order to glimpse the deeper truth about it. *Please read this as my disclaimer. What is written in this book can only be understood intuitively.* Because it cannot be proven, I share this as my personal view of life and this universe. I do not claim to be right, and I leave it to you to take it or leave it.

Also, this is probably a good place to give proper credit to my spirit guides, who have disclosed the ideas in this book. Because I am primarily claircognizant (explained in detail in Chapter V), the information comes through as chunks of ideas, not as dictation. After they send me the information,

I have to unzip the energetic files, translate them to human language, and organize them in a linear manner to be read as paragraphs. Therefore, all credits really belong to my spirit guides. If, on the other hand, there are any parts that are unclear or confusing—my apologies. I have worked hard to do a good job in passing on their messages, but being a human, I am not perfect.

I don't do old-fashioned channeling, in which the medium lets the spirit use their body. This is why there are very few "I" statements in this book. The messages are presented in narratives, not as spirit speaking to you through me.

Two reasons why spiritual writings often sound ambiguous

Spiritual writings often sound ambiguous and confusing. There are two basic reasons:

1. Our ambiguous existence

As we will explore in Chapter I, we exist on two interrelated but different levels. As spirit, we are One. We are already whole and perfect. There is nothing personal on this level. At the same time, we exist as individuals. As such, each one of us is unique and special. We appear to be separate and assume specific personal perspectives.

For this reason, we need to be careful from which level we are discussing any given topic. In this book, I have made sure that the perspective is clear in all discussions.

2. The nature of language

Different people may mean different things when they use the same word, and different words may mean essentially the same thing. For example, I use the word "enlightenment" as the state of being we experience when we disidentify with the ego. It is a state of serene joy because when we disidentify with the ego and realize who we really are, we get to see things as they are without the often pessimistic commentaries of the ego. Others, however, may use different words for the same state of being, such as "awakening," "transcendence," "living in the now," and so on.

Moreover, some people may use the word "enlightenment" to mean something else. This can be confusing, but I am not against any use of words. We just need to be clear what we mean when we use certain words in the context. In this book, extra attention has been paid to clarify the meaning of words. Yet language has its limitations. It is a slow and potentially misleading communication tool. Often, we read through the filter of our own internalized knowledge and judgments, which limits our own understanding. I simply ask the wise readers to be as open-minded as possible.

The structure of this book

We delve into the core of the issue in Chapter I, *The Greater Reality beyond Reality*. This is the foundation of this book and explains how we have come into being and the true nature of life and reality. We also examine the nature of free will and start exploring why bad things happen to good people. Some of the ideas here may sound foreign at first, but please be patient. Hopefully, it will make more sense as you read the following chapters.

Chapter II, *The Truth of the Individual Soul*, examines the nature of our individuality and distinguishes the soul from the ego. While Oneness is wonderful, our individuality is also great. Celebrating individuality is not egotistical—there is a definitive difference between the individual soul and the ego.

Now that we are clear about what the soul is, we review its life beyond physical incarnations in Chapter III, *The Soul's Life beyond Birth and Death*. We will see how reincarnation works and demystify the idea of karma. Further, we explore what it may mean to end the cycle of reincarnation.

The universal energy is loving, wise, and empowering. We examine each of these three qualities in Chapter IV, *Practicing Love*, Chapter V, *The Infinite Wisdom Within*, and Chapter VI, *Courage to Be Powerful*. In Chapter IV, we review what love really means, why we are attracted to certain people, and how self-love relates with love for others. We will also see the power of gratitude. In Chapter V, we explore how we can develop intuition, through which superconscious wisdom comes. The way to read your own Akashic Records is also covered here. Chapter VI releases you from various emotional baggage so that you can live fully empowered.

Chapter VII, *Surfing through Life*, explores how we can live along with the flow of life, not against. It examines the often misunderstood idea of the Law of Attraction and how letting go helps you ride the waves of life with joy and a sense of adventure.

The last chapter, Chapter VIII, *You Are the Living Miracle*, reviews how all the points connect and what it really means to realize Oneness. It is not just a good idea. It is not a goal. We will see how everyone is one's extended self and how everything happens.

Some chapters include short stories I wrote, inspired by my spirit guides, to illustrate the ideas. I hope you enjoy them.

While putting my spirit guides' messages to words has been quite challenging, writing this book has also been a huge delight. Every time I thought I was at the end of my wit and energy, my spirit guides nurtured me, encouraged me, and pointed out—so correctly—that it isn't about me; it is about helping people remember. I hope the words resonate deep within you so that you remember what you once knew ... the reason why you chose to be born.

Love, Light, and Truth,
Akemi G

THE GREATER REALITY
BEYOND REALITY

Reality is merely an illusion,
albeit a very persistent one.
— Albert Einstein

We come from the Source

First there was energy—nothing but the primordial energy. So this energy was whole and complete. Because there was only this energy and not even a single spot that was not this energy, there was no way to measure density, distance, duration, or anything else. Therefore, there was neither time nor space. In a sense, there was nothing.

Then the split. Scientists call it the Big Bang. The primordial energy started to take individual forms, so now, let's call the original chunk of energy the "Source." The Source split in a way that didn't diminish itself. The individualized pieces of the Source have the same innate quality of the original. They are like the cells that divide from the original mother cell. They all have the same DNA even though they develop to look and work quite differently. Some call this the holographic nature of the universe.

Some pieces of the Source became stars. Some planets. Yet others became the inhabitants of the planets or the things that comprise the planets. There is nothing in this universe that is not made of the original Source energy. Because we all come from the Source, we have the same innate quality, or energetic DNA, even though each of us has developed to have unique characteristics. You are one of such individualized extensions of the Source.

Because we are all made of essentially the same energy, we can say there is only one existence in the universe, whether you call it the Source, or the Universal Consciousness, or One

Life, or God. Such a nondualistic view is certainly valid, and we will get back to this point in the last chapter of this book.

At the same time, our individualized lives are also true. We exist on two levels. On the spiritual or energetic level, we are all One. There is only One being in the universe. On the perceptual level, we are individuals. The perceptual level of existence is what we usually call reality, so the energetic level can be called the greater reality. When we discuss spiritual issues, we need to be clear which level we are talking about.

Some people say the perceptual world is only an illusion. In a sense, it is, but the illusion is a meaningful one because the Source split with a purpose.

Our ultimate purpose

The Source energy is not plain waves. It has intelligence. It is aware of itself. And this is the reason why the split happened: while the Source was aware of itself as a wholesome, complete being, it knew so only as an abstract idea. It had no way of knowing so through experience because there was nothing else but itself. The only solution was to split itself so that, however illusionary it may be, there would be something that appeared to be different from itself.

Therefore, our ultimate purpose is to have experiences so that we realize we are One—One being of perfect harmony. In our everyday language, we call it love. On the surface, it may appear that many experiences undermine love, but in the big picture, every experience leads to love one way or another.

Even crimes lead us to love by reminding us of the precious-ness of love. (This, of course, is not an endorsement of crime. We can remember love without painful experiences.) When all the experiences of all the pieces of the Source are put together, we realize our wholeness and perfection.

We are One in spirit, omnipresent and all-knowing, and at the same time, we are individual souls, each with unique attributes. Individuality requires choice, which results in unevenness. As spirit, we have all the qualities within, but as individualized souls, each of us chooses to be one way or another. Physicality further defines the choices. For example, we exist at all places in the universe as spirit, but when a soul incarnates in a physical body, it must choose to be at one location.

Whereas there is only love in the greater reality, in our so-called reality, there is now love and non-love, or the lack of love, just so that we can experience what love feels like in comparison to the lack thereof. This reality is like a giant simu-lation game. We ourselves, as spirit, started this simulation game of individuality and separation so that we might expe-rience that our essence is love and we are whole and perfect.

The intention of this game is good and the setup is flawless. One might argue the setup is too flawless—the illusion is so convincing that it's very easy to believe in the idea of scar-city and limitation and, therefore, the myth that one can win at someone else's loss. This is a challenging game; it is worth spending many lifetimes on it.

The purpose of this life simulation game, then, can be paraphrased as: to realize Oneness while still taking the individualized forms; to experience our innate love in the world of phenomena where non-love feels real.

Reality as a virtual reality simulation

The terms "spirit" and "soul" are often used interchangeably. Sometimes, spirit means non-incarnated soul. In the last section, when I wrote, "We are One in spirit, omnipresent and all-knowing, and at the same time, we are individual souls, each with unique attributes," spirit means the energy prior to individuation, which is also called the Higher Self.

So the terms "Higher Self" and "soul" are sometimes used interchangeably as well. However, Higher Self is a term that focuses on our Oneness. So there is only one Higher Self. Your Higher Self and my Higher Self are ultimately the same. Think of it as one giant being with many faces, which may appear as many entities. Souls, in contrast, are individualized energy. Our soul is our essence that lives on beyond a physical lifetime.

Using the analogy of a virtual reality simulation game, the Higher Self is the designer of the game. But just as you yourself cannot be in the computer game, the Higher Self cannot be in the virtual reality life game. So the Higher Self creates avatars—the individual souls. Each soul has a unique set of attributes and keeps its own history. While the Higher Self knows all the possibilities of the life simulation game as the designer, each soul doesn't consciously remember exactly what happens in the simulation game. Each soul acts as if it is an independent entity, unaware of the overall design of the game. This only makes the game more fun.

The word "game" might make some people think that life is unimportant. Nothing can be further from the truth. Life is a serious game, and we want to do our best in this game. At the same time, relaxation and a sense of humor are also indispensable. A good game player intuitively understands this seeming contradiction.

Some people think life is a school. Because we forget many things at birth, life does seem like a series of learning experiences, and I used to subscribe to this idea, too. However, as we have seen, we are already whole and complete on the spiritual level. We already know love deep within. Therefore, it's not really about learning new lessons but remembering what we know through experiences. Knowing absolute love as spirit is one thing while exploring its endless manifestations in this world of phenomena is quite another. And this is why all spiritual learning feels like remembering, rather than learning something completely new. A great teacher or book can serve only as a reminder.

Again, you are both the Higher Self and the soul. As the individuated soul, you see the world from your specific perspective, and you have your history of experiences. As the Higher Self, you know how all the experiences, your own and everyone else's, fit into the big picture.

Theater plays and dreams:
How it has been explained historically

Viewing reality as a virtual reality game like one we play on a computer is not a new idea. There was even a popular movie based loosely on this idea. Before computers came out, people worldwide and throughout history used other analogies to explain the same.

In *As You Like It*, William Shakespeare wrote, "All the world's a stage, And all the men and women merely players." We are like actors who come onto the stage. There is a greater reality beyond the stage, and we are only taking on various roles in the play for the time being. The play is not ultimately real, but it's useful to experience something.

The Bible states Adam fell asleep but never explicitly says he woke up. It is possible that this implies the ancient people's view that this reality is a dream, which means they sensed the existence of the greater reality beyond the dream. I heard Hindus have a similar view, that this reality is only the dream of Shiva, the one consciousness.

Further, Tao is a closely related idea to Akasha. Lao Tzu wrote in the first chapter of *Tao Te Ching*, "The tao that can be told is not the eternal Tao. The name that can be named is not the eternal Name. The unnamable is the eternally real. Naming is the origin of all particular things." The unnamable, eternally real Tao forms into all particular things that can be named. (Tao also means the way of life based on its understanding.)

There are probably many other traditions that describe the same truth using different words and different analogies. Somehow we knew this for a long time. We are like children playing a make-believe game. We are in the story we ourselves are creating.

The Akashic Records

Because we are One in spirit, there is no secret on the spiritual level. Every soul knows everything about every other soul through their multiple lifetimes. This knowledge, or the energetic records of all memories, is called the Akashic Records.

In Sanskrit, the primordial energy of the Source is called Akasha. All four elements—earth, water, fire, and air—come from Akasha and eventually return to Akasha. So we can say that we all come from Akasha and return to Akasha. (Because Akasha fills all spaces, it also means space or sky.)

Everything that has ever happened since the original split and everything that can possibly happen in the future is recorded. The Akashic Records are often thought to be the energetic records of all souls' pasts, presents, and futures, but they contain far more. They also contain our collective wisdom that we have accumulated through all the experiences.

The Akashic Records are available to everyone. All it takes is to open our hearts and let ourselves remember. (More on this in Chapter V.) What is shared in this book is gathered from the Akashic Records. I hope it resonates in you—that is to say, that the words in this book help you remember what you always knew but may have forgotten.

At the same time, it doesn't matter if someone believes any of the information here. Some people say they don't believe in the spiritual stuff, and in the end, this is fine. We—every single one of us, including those who don't believe—are spiritual anyway. Just as gravity always works whether someone believes in it or not, we are spiritual, energetic beings anyway. It's just helpful when we understand how it works.

God in human image

This book is meant to be spiritual but not necessarily religious. Religions have been both great blessings and the causes of serious conflicts. I do not intend to deny any religions because I know there are many paths to truth, and all paths that lead to truth are valid. Some people do find God in a religion, so rejecting religion is counterproductive. Others, however, find divinity in nature, art, or everyday life, and this is certainly a great approach.

The way I see it is that God is the Source, the universal energy that gave birth to all existences and keeps giving birth. As we have seen, this energy is intelligent and its fundamental nature is love. So we can say God is love and love is God, and God is omnipresent and all-knowing.

Visualizing the Source, the pure energy, is somewhat challenging, however. The energy doesn't have its own image but keeps changing its appearance. So we imagined God to be in human form. As long as this image is helpful, this is fine. The potential problem is that we might start thinking of God to be like someone we know, which is how the image of a judgmental, angry, and vengeful God started. It really isn't about God but about the people who abuse the word "God."

If you like the image of a human-like God, whether it is male or female or gender-neutral, you might want to envision God as humble and tolerant. God, or the Source, becomes everyone, including the poorest among us, the sickest among us, and the most dissolute among us, so humility is certainly its quality. God grants us free will, knowing all the potential problems we may cause with it, so God is tolerant. In fact, it would be hard for anyone to be more humble and tolerant than God.

God is the Source energy that has brought forth the whole world of phenomena, so we can say God is older than the universe. The human image of God, however, is quite new. Regardless, as long as a religious teaching promotes greater love, it is in accordance with the truth.

The critical nature of free will

"If God exists, why does he let all the bad things happen?" is a common question. If we define God as someone who started this giant life simulation game—in other words, the personalized image of the Source—then God must allow everything to happen. This is called free will.

Free will is not about having one's way and fulfilling every whim as we please. Free will is our right and responsibility to choose from the many options in this life simulation game. Just as in a computer game, the virtual reality game of life presents options—you can go right or left or keep going straight forward, for example. Depending on the choice you make, life presents you another set of choices—and another, and another.

We started this game in order to realize love through our experiences. In order for love to be love, it must be chosen freely. Forced love is not love. Likewise, forced harmony is not harmony, and forced peace is not peace. We need to voluntarily and freely choose. So there are choices for non-love (such as hatred and indifference) as well as for love, choices for disruption and disorder as well as for harmony, choices for violence as well as for peace. This way, we are fully prepared to choose.

If God acted like a cop or a bossy supervisor and prevented us from doing certain things, we would not know the glory of love, which is what life is all about. Needless to say, God knows this and therefore honors our free will—even the free will to criticize God. As humans, our perception is often shortsighted, and sometimes we see only the troubles free will can cause, but this doesn't mean free will itself is no good.

In fact, attempting to limit or control others' free will is the most counterproductive thing we can do. This is what "devils" do in the traditional stories; they trick and manipulate others' free will, usually with a promise of giving something that the person desperately desires. And if we define a devil as a being who interferes with free will, then we realize devils are not necessarily dark monsters. Some devils may look impressively beautiful and others may sound overly kind. (There is nothing wrong with beauty or kindness, of course. It is the manipulation that is wrapped pretty or disguised as kindness that is the problem.) Please note this is not a condemnation of anyone. Any soul can choose to quit the interference anytime, just as they can choose to continue doing so.

Because of free will, there is neither hell nor a big judgment. If God gives and honors free will, of course he or she is not going to judge our choices. In effect, judgment would limit the free will. If you know certain actions will send you to hell and you choose to avoid those actions, is your choice to not do them truly free?

The question, "If God exists, why does he let all the bad things happen?" is also about how we view experiences. Often, what we call "bad things" or problems are our opportunities to realize our inner love, wisdom, and power. We are given such challenges because we are entrusted to handle them. We will review this point in more detail in Chapter VI.

It is also essential to realize that our judgment of what is happening in our life is quite superficial. In a sense, bad things never happen. We only think a certain situation is bad. Life is never against you because you are the one who is creating it. Everything happens for you, and we will revisit this perspective in Chapter VIII.

There is no original sin

The Bible teaches that our ancestors committed the original sin by betraying God and eating from the tree of knowledge of good and evil, which resulted in our "fall" or separation from God. When we understand that our reality started with the Source's intention to know itself and the resulting split to create the illusion of separation, this story can be seen in a new light.

Without the polarity, the Source could not know its perfection. It is the Source's full intention to have this reality that contains both good and evil so that we can choose with our free will. Adam and Eve did just that. What is called the original sin is not a sin at all; it is about the courage we take to exercise our free will, which is anticipated by God. The all-knowing God knew they were going to eat from that tree and let them. The rest of the story about Adam and Eve leaving Eden is figurative talk about how souls leave the spirit world and come to this world of phenomena.

Life is not a punishment but an adventure. It may not always feel good, but that is the whole point, that we cannot experience the glory without also experiencing the challenges. It is only when we are wrapped up with the judgmental ego that we are left feeling bitter, resenting the so-called original sin.

Nature of time

Time doesn't really exist. We observe time only because we live in the physicality, which has a built-in speed limit. Time, however, helps us to experience life in an organized manner. Rather than everything happening all at once, we can experience one thing after another in the seeming flow of time. This helps us experience cause and effect.

On the spiritual plane, where we are not limited by physicality, time doesn't flow one-way, so effect can precede cause. For example, if cause must precede effect, we'd have a question, and then we'd do the research and thinking to reach an answer. But have you ever conceived a question with the feeling that the answer already exists? The answer may not be clear yet, so we do the research and other work to clarify it—not to produce the answer but only to remember it.

Does this mean the future already exists? Yes. However, there are many futures, not just one. Life is not like walking down the road and meeting the predetermined events. The analogy of computer games is useful again here. In such games, depending on the choice you make in the current situation, a new scene opens. Then you make another decision, which again leads to the next scene. There are so many choices and so many possible scenes in the life simulation that it almost feels infinite. This is what it means to create one's own life with our free will.

The possibilities are not really infinite, however. Just as all the possible combinations in a computer game are determined when it is designed, all the possibilities of this reality are already set. It's just that, with so many options, we are better off paying attention to the available choices rather than worrying about whether or not the desired outcome is possible. If you can clearly envision the outcome, it is possible—that's why you can envision it.

Can we miss the available options in front of us? Very much so. We often don't notice what is physically in front of our eyes, and choices are far easier to miss. This is why we need to cultivate our imagination, our ability to see what is possible.

The one-way flow of time in this physical reality also helps us to live our life as it happens. If we could freely go back to the past, many people would go back to the time that they think they made a mistake in order to fix it. This, however, wouldn't necessarily change their present life as they expected, so they'd go back again ... and again to fix the past. The end result is that they'd literally be living in the past rather than living their current life for new adventures.

When we open up to see all the available choices and choose with loving awareness, we move through the life simulation more smoothly and with more joy. Synchronicity happens often, which is nothing more than events lining up as they were originally intended.

God was a great storyteller ...

This reality is an illusion within the greater reality. However, illusion doesn't mean it is worthless. On the contrary, it is a great illusion that brought all of us into existence. It is the illusion that makes the adventure of life possible by working like a giant simulation game.

We—not only humans, but every existence in this universe—exist on two interrelated levels. In the greater reality, or on the spiritual or energetic level, everything already is. There is only now, and there is only one perfect existence. It's the world of "being." In the so-called reality, or on the perceptual level, we appear in various shapes and colors and always in the process of "becoming." Everything is a work-in-progress and dreaming perfection. It's the world of experience. Both worlds are meaningful and beautiful. Each depends on the other.

We are the director of the movie while also the actors in it. As actors, each of us chooses what role to play. For example, I chose the role of Akemi, and you chose the role of you. We then continue to choose, refining our roles. We are also the director, who creates and organizes this reality. This doesn't mean we are authorized to act like a cranky control freak. The creation happens within us, not by manipulating others—there are no "others" for the director. The movie that we are creating and playing is a form of illusion, but it's useful to experience certain things.

As long as we are aware that this reality is an illusion, the illusion is not a problem—we can even enjoy it. It becomes a problem only when we think this is the only reality, and it is a problem because it is incorrect. An incorrect premise leads us to incorrect assumptions, resulting in sufferings. When we remember there is the greater reality beyond this reality, we remember we are not just actors but also the creative director.

Here is yet another way to illustrate the nature of this so-called reality.

God was a great storyteller. All the stories were marvelous, exciting, unexpected ... some exceedingly courageous, some exquisitely beautiful ....

Souls just couldn't get enough of the stories. "Tell us more!" they begged. "Please, more!"

God never told exactly the same story twice.

Finally, God gently asked, "Would you like to be in the stories, rather than just listening to them?"

"Can we do that? Oh, my! That would be terrific!" the souls replied.

And so we came to being.

THE TRUTH OF THE INDIVIDUAL SOUL

We are not human beings
having a spiritual experience.
We are spiritual beings
having a human experience.
— Pierre Teilhard de Chardin

We don't change

Individuality is wonderful. It is how we realize our purpose of love. If I don't exist as an individual and you also don't exist as an individual, how can we experience love of any kind?

As we reviewed in Chapter I, we exist on two levels at the same time. As spirit, we are One. As individuated souls, we are individuals. As spirit, we are already whole and perfect. We only know love for everything, and non-love doesn't even exist. While this absolute existence is great, there is no way to know its greatness because there is no reference point. This is why we split and exist as individuals. Oneness is wonderful and so is individuality. The two levels don't negate each other; each level supports the other.

Each individuated piece of the Source assumes its own unique perspective and accumulates its own experiences so that, put together, we'd know what it is to be whole and in harmony. So each soul has its own characteristics and keeps its own history through many lifetimes. This means that the universe relies on you to be you. Without you being you, the universe is not complete.

Therefore, our essential personality does not change. It doesn't need to change. Nobody needs to become somebody that they are not. Believing that we can change ourselves, much less someone else, is a self-defeating myth that the ego entertains. The ego is not the same as the individuated soul. The ego is a false self that we think we are, and we will see how it works in more detail later in this chapter.

What we can change is our choices. This life is a giant simulation game, and choosing different options brings different results, leading to different experiences. We, as souls, spend many lifetimes experimenting with various choices. Free will allows us to do this.

For example, if you are high on the sensitivity spectrum, that won't change. You cannot become less sensitive. You can, however, choose your environment. You don't need to stay where you feel insecure. You can also choose to utilize your sensitivity. Expressed well, you will be perceived as a kind, nurturing person rather than an easily hurt, insecure person. You might also do well in the arts—another choice you can make.

If, on the other hand, you are low on the sensitivity scale, you cannot become more sensitive. What you can do is choose to listen to what people say and learn what offends sensitive people and what delights them. Or you can choose to ignore them as nonsense just because you don't understand. That is within your choice.

The catch of self-improvement

The well-intended aspiration of improving oneself has a catch that few seem to note. It implies that you need to be improved. But what kind of serious character defects do you really have? And why do you want to improve yourself? To be loved and accepted? Can't we be loved as we are? Isn't that what unconditional love means?

The only valid reason for self-improvement is the desire to experience our inner divinity. Whether you are religious or not, deep inside, you remember the perfection of the Source, which some of us choose to call God. And we yearn to manifest this greatness that is deep within us, like a hidden jewel waiting to shine. This is what drives, for example, musicians to practice their instruments more, even when they sound excellent to average ears. They are trying to manifest their innermost perfection. Artists attempt to make this hidden greatness visible. Athletes push their physical limits in the same way.

We also resonate when we see this inner divinity in others. This is why we spontaneously yell, "Yes!" when we see outstanding performances and cry when we see out-of-this-world beauty. Such experiences remind us of the perfection of ourselves as spirit.

Unfortunately, self-improvement is usually about finding faults in oneself, rather than the greatness, and trying to fix them. When we want to find faults, we never fail. You are either too uptight and need to learn how to relax or too lazy and need to learn productivity tips. You are either too reserved and need to open up to love or too much of a people-pleaser and need to learn how to set up boundaries. You are either too arrogant and need to learn respect for others or too insecure and need to build confidence. The list goes on and on. You may even find yourself at both ends of the spectrum, for example, worrying too much about details sometimes and not being careful enough at other times.

There is no end to the problems you can find. The ego likes to find faults and then agonize over them. The ego makes you feel as if your life will be wonderful when you achieve just this one improvement, but this is never true. After a temporary contentment, the ego finds yet another problem to work on. And did you really change? No, you just changed superficially. Our essential personality is sustained throughout the soul's long life. This is why most self-improvements are fundamentally self-defeating.

However, the magical thing about life is that this potentially self-defeating attempt to improve oneself can lead someone to realize their perfection as spirit. There are many paths to this realization and every path is valid—even the ones that involve some deviations.

The ego, or who you think you are

The ego is the collective function of the thinking mind that makes judgments based on past experiences, direct or indirect, for the purpose of survival and self-preservation. Most of us identify with the ego rather than the soul, not to mention the Higher Self. This is why some say that they want to know what their soul is saying or that they are seeking their soul. The soul is your essence, so there is no need to explore what the soul is saying—that answer is already within. And you will never find your soul anywhere outside yourself. The reason why people think in this line is that they think they are something other than their soul: the ego.

Take a moment and think about how you might answer the question, "Who am I?"

- Your name is not who you are. It's just a tag to identify you. You can change your name, and you are still who you are.

- Your job is not who you are. It's just one of the roles you are currently playing. You can change or lose your job, and you are still who you are.

- Your family status, such as being a mother, is not who you are. This is another role you are playing. Before you assumed that role, you were you.

- Your nationality, ethnicity, social group, religious affiliation, and so on are not who you are. These are groups you belong to. Your affiliation may characterize you socioculturally, but you are not just a group member.

- Your body is not who you are. It is your current vehicle. You are the one inhabiting the body.

- Your history is not who you are. You are the one who created your experiences, and you are not the results of your experiences.

- Your thoughts are not who you are. You are the one who is thinking. Your thoughts belong to you, but they are not who you are.

As you may have noticed, this question is hard to answer. In truth, it is impossible to answer because who you are is bigger than any answer. If you can accept the indescribable nature of your true identity, you unveil the mystery of life. Often, however, we choose an easier answer that sounds good enough.

The ego is that image of self, which is usually the combination of the aforementioned answers. (The term "self" is often used synonymously with the ego. Because most of us identify with the ego, this works fine. However, I stay away from using the term "Self" to mean the soul or the Higher Self because it is too confusing with the term "self.")

Although the ego works as if it is an independent entity, it is not. It is only the collection of ideas and the way we think. It is empty. It is quite convenient to discuss the ego as if it is a personality, but in truth, it has no life, just as the collection of light beams on a screen has no life even though the image may appear lively. Because the ego is actually empty, it keeps us busy with anything and everything in order to prevent us from looking into the ego itself. Once we really look into the ego, we will notice we are not the ego, and the ego loses its power to run our life.

It is a common myth that we need to kill the ego to be enlightened. However, it is impossible to kill the ego because the ego doesn't have a life. It is only the identification with the ego that is untrue and therefore problematic. When we understand the ego, we understand that it has been helping us to survive in this physical world by making quick judgments, which is useful in emergency situations. We don't need to get rid of the ego. We just need to disidentify with it.

Five ways to disidentify with the ego

There are many ways to disidentify with the ego, to realize that you are not the ego that you have thought you are. Let us take a look at some of the major approaches:

1. Through meditation

Meditation is not about what you do. It's about the state of being in which you calm down enough to observe your thoughts rather than chase them. The ego constantly keeps us occupied with thoughts. It is its main tactic to distract us so that we don't notice we are not the ego. Therefore, by not chasing the thoughts, we spontaneously disidentify with the ego. At first, you will find your mind very busy with all kinds of thoughts. Just watch them without chasing or trying to suppress them. Eventually one thought disappears, but another shows up immediately. Again, just watch it pass by. There's no need to force it to go away. It will go away if you don't do anything with it.

At some point, you find yourself in a space void of thoughts and words—a very quiet space but not the dead kind of quiet. It's filled with lively joy. Stay there as long as you like. You might find yet another thought sneaking in—no need to panic. Just watch it disappear.

Having said that meditation is not about how you do it, many people have found certain methods helpful in the process of calming the mind while being clearly awake. Whether sitting on the floor or in a chair, you want to keep your spine straight yet relaxed. (This is important for your physical health as well.

The head is quite heavy, so if you lean forward or back, your back, especially the lower back, receives unnatural pressure.) If you are sitting on the floor, you might want to prop up your buttocks so that your hip joints are not strained. If you are sitting in a chair, choose a firm and stable chair. It's a good idea to wear loose clothes. You don't have to do it indoors— meditation in a quiet garden or in nature is delightful. Just be sure the sun is not directly in your eyes and you are unlikely to be disturbed by loud noise.

Although you can meditate anywhere, anytime, you might find it helpful to practice at about the same time, in the same location. This conditions your subconscious so that you can get into a meditative state with relative ease. Elements of rituals, such as burning incense or chanting before meditation, may also be helpful.

There are basically two approaches in meditation. One is to focus on just one thing, maybe a candle light or your own breath or one word / sound (mantra), so that others fade away. The other is not to focus on anything and just release all obses- sions. Eventually, you will be sitting there, knowing you are there, sensing what is going on in and around you, but you have no thoughts. That is the state of meditation.

In other words, the best meditation experience is one in which you feel as if you don't exist. You find yourself void of all thoughts and intentions. Not even the efforts of clearing thoughts or calming down are there. No nothing. It's the state of complete relaxation in which you realize you are One with all.

Discussing the various methods of meditation in detail is out of the scope of this book, and there are already many good books about them. Just keep things simple. Again, meditation is not about how you do it. It's about the state of being in which you find yourself.

Also, if you feel calm while meditating but are obsessed at other times, the complete disidentification has not happened yet. When you disidentify with the ego, all of life becomes a form of meditation, whatever you may be doing.

2. Through the experience of love

Because the ego is about survival and self-conservation, it cannot love. The best it can do is put on a nice face as a way to get a favorable deal. True love is about the soul. Therefore, when we truly love, we automatically disidentify with the ego.

Even when love starts as romantic infatuation, which is about the ego, it has a chance to grow into the unconditional love of the soul. It starts as a beautiful yet quite self-centered desire to gain the attention and affection of the other person, and through some mystery of life, it grows to a sincere good-will for the well-being of the beloved, not oneself. At this point, you love everything about the person, including their possible decision to leave you. In true love, no betrayal or disappointment exists.

It's the same with love for family and friends. The relationship doesn't need to be only about the commitment to preserve the family and social connection. It can grow to be something bigger.

We can also experience the disidentification with the ego through the love of art, nature, or any dedicated work. When we forget ourselves in the creation or enjoyment of art, we are actually finding our true identity. When we stand speechless at the magnificence of nature, we are experiencing it as the soul. When we work to bring forth something that is bigger than ourselves, we are abandoning the aspects of the ego, and the more the awareness of that experience is sustained, the more we get to know ourselves as who we really are.

Once you completely disidentify with the ego, you stay that way whether you stay with your lover or not. The disidentification is not about them but about yourself. If you feel resentful about the loss of love, I feel for you, but I must say the disidentification didn't happen.

We will further explore the nature of true love in Chapter IV.

3. Through complete service

Because the ego is about self-benefit, we can disidentify with it through thorough service to others. Although it is not about the amount of time and money that is put in, part-time charity probably doesn't get you to the point of disidentifying with the ego. Not all the religious leaders succeed, either. This approach is about serving others past the point where the ego screams, "Oh, no! Helping others is nice, but who is going to help me? I have nothing for myself." There is a reason why Jesus and other teachers kept nothing for themselves. It was their way of freedom.

Closely related to this approach is disidentification through religious dedication. Traditionally, the word "salvation" is used to describe this path of disidentification. Salvation is essentially the same as disidentification with the ego because the ego is the cause of all suffering.

There are basically two approaches in religious salvation. One is to save oneself through your own discipline and resulting awareness. Zen is basically based on this approach. The other is to be saved through complete dedication to deities, such as Christ, who have the power of salvation. Both approaches work because we exist on two levels. Salvation through oneself is about fully realizing your spiritual nature and, therefore, your inner divinity. Salvation through external deity is about living by faith rather than by the ego's judgments and consequently realizing you are not your ego, even while you exist as an individual.

Disidentification through religious dedication is closely related to disidentification through service because one supports the other in most cases. When you completely believe you can be, and indeed are, saved by God, you quit caring about yourself in the ego's signature obsessive way. Your attention shifts to something bigger and service becomes natural. And in order to serve others so selflessly, you probably need some faith, to say the least.

The potential problem with this approach is that it is easy to bring judgment to service and religious dedication. People might judge service by the amount of money donated or time volunteered. Then they would expect to have salvation, or disidentification, when they do a certain amount of work. Expectation is about the ego, however, so this is totally counterproductive. Religious dedication can also be abused by political and religious authorities. History is filled with incidents in which religious leaders manipulated and took advantage of their followers. Many religious leaders are not disidentified with the ego to begin with. Therefore, unless you study your religion through books that are as close to the original as possible, it is easy to misunderstand religion.

The path of service does have an advantage as well. For those who are willing, the path is readily available. No mysterious meditation practice or the object of love is required. There are people in need everywhere, and you can start by helping one of them. Eventually, you arrive at that scary point of the ego's resistance; when you pass that point, you disidentify with the ego. And even if you don't, you help some people in the process.

4. Through beauty

The Source started this reality by splitting itself into many pieces, still essentially being itself. The Source energy is so intelligent that it made the world marvelous and beautiful. When you notice how magically beautiful this reality is, you are identifying with who you really are, the soul. The ego has no real interest in beauty. It's too busy with all the other things.

Nature, the creation beyond human involvement, is a great place to immerse ourselves in beauty. Spend time in nature doing nothing. There is a point in such seemingly leisurely, or even wasteful, time. In a sense, it's a form of meditation while your eyes are wide open. Stand still at the beauty of a sunrise, feel the awe at the greatness of mountains, and forget about time as you watch a tiny bug in a flower. Do this often.

One such moment of beauty may or may not be sufficient to disidentify with the ego. Even after you are significantly moved by beauty and feel you went far away, you may reidentify with the ego when you return to your everyday life. Be gentle yet persistent with yourself. Keep taking time to experience beauty.

At some point, you will make that big departure. It's when the whole world starts brimming with beauty. Then you realize you have hardly been seeing anything. While we identify with the ego, we don't really see—we just glance at things and think we know what we saw. When you disidentify with the ego and start seeing, you find extraordinary beauty in every ordinary thing, and you realize there is no such thing as ordinary.

5. Through suffering

Everyone is going to be enlightened, or get to the point of disidentifying with the ego, sooner or later. Nobody can escape it—it is only a matter of time. We all come from the Source. The Source energy in us is not going to be obsessed with the ego indefinitely. It may or may not happen in this lifetime, but it will happen eventually to everyone.

For those who would like to consciously disidentify with the ego, there are many approaches. Meditation, love, service, and beauty are but a few such approaches. For those who continue to identify with the ego and the drama the ego creates, there is a last resort: suffering. We can say suffering is the default path to enlightenment when we don't opt out with other approaches.

The ego thinks it knows how to survive in this world. It thinks it knows better than the soul. So the ego runs our life most of the time—until something happens that the ego cannot handle with its known tactics. However, the ego will still cling to its control and we will suffer. No events can cause suffering by themselves. It's the ego's resistance that causes the suffering. As long as we identify with the ego, the suffering continues—the ego is suffering from its loss of control. Eventually, we realize we cannot go on like this and let something bigger than the ego take care of the situation.

The potential problem with this approach is that the identification may return once your suffering is over. This means you suffer again. The complete disidentification may come through extremely large suffering or repeated sufferings.

The ego that criticizes the ego

There are many ways to disidentify with the ego, and as pointed out earlier, all paths that lead you to the destination are good. Also, please note that the process of disidentification may take awhile, or it may happen in a moment of grace.

What we want to stay away is the path that appears to be valid but is not. Analyzing the ego in contrast to the soul and pretending to be more like the soul is one such misguided path. Learning the characteristics of the ego and trying to catch yourself when you are thinking like the ego does not let you disidentify with the ego. In fact, the harder you try this approach, the more you reinforce your identification with the ego because analysis and criticism are functions of the ego.

The ego is cunning and it can split into two—the regular ego and the ego that has learned the spiritual lingo and now criticizes the regular ego. The latter is still the ego, no matter how wise it may sound. The soul doesn't criticize. It doesn't know how. The soul knows only to love. While the ego criticizes everything, including the ego itself, the soul watches it with loving amusement.

In other words, we cannot disidentify with the ego by pretending to think and act like the soul. If you are trying to think and act like the soul, you are in fact identifying with the ego, and this is the very reason you are trying to be more like the soul. In truth, you are already the soul. No trying is required.

For example, when you try to be more loving because love is the quality of the soul, you are reinforcing your identification with the ego—and that love is not love at all. Love with any agenda, even the noble-sounding agenda to be enlightened, ceases to be love. Genuine love just is, with no agenda. Only the ego, not the soul, confuses true love and fake love and tries to be more loving.

Likewise, when you try to stay away from power because power is the quality often associated with the ego, you are in effect identifying with the ego. Power is a dirty word only to the ego. Other people's power is worrisome to your ego, who wants to have its way, and power acquired by your ego fattens it up, which also leads to suffering soon enough. In contrast, the soul is always connected to the highest power in the universe: the Source. The soul has the power that cannot be lost. The soul, then, freely chooses whether such power is to be used in a worldly manner or not.

So stop educating your ego. The ego can never know the soul because it is only a collection of thoughts and judgments. Even though it acts like a personality, the ego is really empty. It feels like a personality only because you identify with it and give it life, so to say. The ego, therefore, has no access to truly understand the soul or the vastness of the Source. You are already the soul, so rather than intellectualizing what the soul may be like, just drop your misguided identification with the ego.

Ego as the isolated fearful child

Even though the soul has individuality, it is still aware of its connection to one another and to the Source. Souls know one another and are at peace with other souls. The ego, on the other hand, is cut off—it is only a collection of thoughts and judgments after all. Because the ego is limited in its knowing, it compares oneself to others in its attempt to figure out its place among others. Then the ego thinks it is either better or worse than others. In other words, the ego views others either as a burden or a threat.

So the ego builds walls around itself to protect itself from such perceived burden or threat, making the ego even more isolated. At this point, meditation can become yet another thing to boast about and so is service. The ego probably pays only intellectual respect to beauty. Love can be a pathway to salvation, and sure enough, the ego craves love—or more accurately, to be loved. The ego can love only for the sake of being loved, so most of the time it finds faults in the lover before the love grows to the selfless level. This is why suffering is the path to disidentification for many people.

When we notice how miserable our life is because of our identification with the ego and its judgments, controls, and defensiveness, it's easy to hate the ego. But again, this is only a false disidentification. The soul cannot hate. The soul knows only to love.

Although the ego may seem like a tyrant, it is more helpful to think of it as a fearful child. It is easily frightened, even by the shadows on the wall. It cries often and throws tantrums—if it's not bragging that it's the king or queen of the world. Its worldview is limited and skewed. But would you hate such a child? No. You'd take care of it with love.

When you love and care for the ego, you are disidentifying with the ego; that is to say, you know you are not the ego. You are the soul caring for the ego. The ego then can be helpful in certain situations in which you need to react quickly for survival, such as when you see someone with a gun.

Thinking is a useful tool

When you understand how the ego controls your life by obsessively projecting thoughts, you might think that thinking is no good. Not so. Thinking is a highly useful tool, just as the body is a useful tool to get things done in the physical world. The point is that, as with any tool, you want to put it down when you are done using it. Use your thinking faculty when you are working on a math puzzle or your business plan. Then, when you are done, put the thoughts to rest. You are not your thoughts, not your thinking mind—you are the one who is utilizing the thinking mind.

Likewise, knowledge is wonderful as long as we know what it is about. We can observe, experiment, analyze, theorize, and so on to accumulate knowledge. Then from this pool of knowledge, we can build various useful gadgets or write interesting books. Knowledge, however, can never get you to experience the truth of your soul and its connection to the Source. That experience of knowing can come directly to you only when you disidentify with the ego and all the knowledge it is holding on to.

Delightful serenity

The benefit of disidentifying with the ego cannot be described in words. You suddenly find yourself in a clean, serene space. However, it is not a lifeless tranquility. It is filled with vibrant joy. You suddenly realize you are free. There's no need to free yourself; you've been free all the time. It was only your own ego that was making it appear otherwise. You realize you don't have to solve your problems. Most problems evaporate on their own, and you understand that the few that are left are challenges in the life simulation game, something that you wholeheartedly tackle as you would do in a sport game.

You feel that everything—people, animals, plants, mountains, the sea, and even the city buildings—are all interconnected and One. It's an invisible yet sure connection that is not affected by what you or anyone might do. You feel the one heart beating in everyone and everything. You realize you are part of the one big life, one consciousness.

Further, you realize what "living in the now" really means. It is not about the denial of the past and the future, or the concept of linear time. You find yourself in this now, which is fresh and beautiful, which is so undeniably sure and solid. It's like the whole world suddenly gains a new layer of colors.

You also realize that, in this Oneness that is complete and perfect, the individual you is uniquely imperfect, and your unique imperfection is the perfect contribution you make to the whole.

So as you enjoy the delightful serenity of Oneness, you can also enjoy this giant life simulation game, or the phenomenon of individuality.

THE SOUL'S LIFE BEYOND BIRTH AND DEATH

Birth is not a beginning;
death is not an end.
— Chuang Tzu

Death is not the opposite of birth

Our current understanding of life is grossly limited. When we see only our physical body and the thoughts our brain produces, birth appears to be the beginning and death the end. However, when we understand that our essence is the soul, we see that both birth and death are points of transformation and relocation in the soul's life. They are not opposite but, in fact, quite similar events. When you die, you leave your physical body and move to the other side. When you were born, you came to this side and took on a physical form. If you think death is scary, please know birth is a pretty daring endeavor as well. Although most of us don't consciously remember, you probably have been through multiple births and deaths already.

There are benefits to keeping one physical lifetime within a reasonable period and resting on the other side in between lifetimes. In many of us, the emotional load of life eventually becomes overwhelming. This affects our physical body, and the deterioration of the physical body further adds to the emotional burden. We are all here to experience love, but when our feelings become so conditioned with previous experiences and the body grows weak as a result, it becomes hard to have new experiences with freshness and openness. So we opt out.

It's like taking a break when you play a computer game. You don't need to complete the game in one sitting. You can take a break, and when you come back, you resume where you left off. In the meantime, you can contemplate how you might want to play the game differently next time. When you resume the game, you are still the same you, but you choose a different appearance. This is what reincarnation is about.

How souls choose their birth settings

First, please note that no soul incarnates by chance. The way you were conceived may have been planned or accidental, and you may or may not have felt wanted, but on the soul level, your incarnation was planned. You chose to be here for a reason.

In this giant simulation game of life, you have the free will to choose your birth settings. It is helpful to experience this physical world from various perspectives, so we tend to choose a different location, different social status, and different gender when we plan our rebirth. You can also choose a parent—mother or father, or possibly both. This is not a set-in-stone rule, however. For example, the already incarnated soul that a newly rebirthing soul wishes to choose as its mother may be physiologically too old or otherwise unfit for pregnancy. In such cases, the soul may choose to be born as her grandchild or other relative. Or it may postpone this relationship for a later incarnation and choose another candidate for now.

The reasons a soul may choose to be related to another soul are many. It is not always about liking that soul, as the word "like" usually means. Sometimes there is unfinished business from past lives, and they need to play out a certain scenario. For example, think of a soul who was married to a man who was not a bad person but had many affairs. They essentially loved each other, but their idea of marriage was vastly different; therefore their relationship was difficult. In the following lifetime, the husband may be incarnated as a woman, and the wife may choose her as her mother. This way, they can learn to appreciate each other in a new setting, free from sexual heat. The soul that was unhappy as the wife might appreciate the other soul as its mother for its open-minded, nurturing nature.

Souls even choose their former enemies as parents. It's not about revenge, of course. The objective of a life setting is always about enhancing the opportunities to experience love.

Life theme

While our ultimate purpose is to experience love and, therefore, to remember our infinitely loving, divine nature, this ultimate purpose is so large that we break it down into smaller, more manageable pieces that focus on one aspect of love, such as generosity, authenticity, or lightheartedness. I call this the life theme. Each soul chooses one main life theme and a few secondary life themes for the upcoming incarnation. Life theme is another factor souls take into consideration when they choose birth settings and make an overall life plan.

The way souls choose their life themes and make their life plans according to the themes is extremely wise. It is far beyond the shortsightedness of the ego. For example, a soul might choose lightheartedness as the new theme because it realizes it has been far too serious and strict—to the point that the natural flow of love was interrupted. This soul, then, might choose to be born into a family with very traditional, rigid values. The parents would teach the opposite of what the soul is trying to experience. They'd teach to obey manners and may even spank their child when the child doesn't follow the conventional rules. There'd be very little laughter at home while the child grows up.

This setup, when accepted for what it is, helps the child to remember the importance of humor and lightheartedness. It's not about blindly denying or rejecting the parents' way. By first experiencing the lack of what the soul seeks to experience, it encourages the soul to actively pursue its life theme of choice.

However, because most of us identify with the ego, which is all about safety and easy survival, you may be tempted to resent your own plan—and of course, you don't remember it was you who chose it to be the way it is.

Further, please note that not all souls set their life themes. There are many souls who simply come to this world to look around and accumulate experiences. Choosing life themes is up to one's free will, and if a soul intends to incarnate with no themes, it does so.

We choose our own destiny

"Anything is possible," sounds good, but countless options can actually be daunting, so the soul sets a certain framework prior to birth. It's not about limiting the choices but about making choices more available. Using the analogy of the computer simulation game, we set the available options and resulting new scenes of our own life prior to birth. This is still a very complicated and sophisticated system of billions and billions of possible combinations. So the soul further chooses a few experiences that it absolutely goes for and several others that are highly desirable yet optional. This way, you can focus on how you connect the chosen points of experiences.

The must-have experiences of life are sometimes called destiny or destiny points. Destiny points are chosen in a way that supports the soul's life themes. While destiny points happen anyway, the details such as when and how they happen, are usually left open. For example, a soul may choose motherhood as a must-have experience. If this is the case, it will happen. The soul may choose to jump into it when she is still a teenager, even though such a pregnancy may be viewed as unconventional. Or she may put it off, and when she is in her forties, she may suddenly realize she must have a child by any means. For other souls, on the other hand, parenthood may be just an optional experience. Their must-have experience may be to serve the world in a certain role or to live in a certain area or something else.

It is important to remember that, even though the terms "must-have experiences" and "destiny points" may sound like they supersede our free will, this is not about obligation and limitation. It is we ourselves, as the souls, who choose such experiences with free will. If you feel limited, it is probably not because of your life plan but because you are not open to all the possibilities, and therefore, you are not really seeing all the available options.

You cannot live someone else's life

Each soul has its own life plan—its personal portion of the life simulation that includes the birth setting, themes, destiny points and more—that it specifically designs to work with its unique characteristics. This means that we cannot live someone else's life. Your parents and other caretakers might want you to live a certain life that they think is appropriate for you, but if that is not what you have chosen on the soul level, it is not going to work. You might try to follow that forced path for a while, only to fail or end up feeling so distressed that you rebel. Either way would bring you back to your own path so that you can at least cover the must-have experiences.

Further, you yourself may be tempted to live the life society endorses as appropriate or safe. This does not work, either. You will feel like a fake, and your life will be difficult and clumsy. Regardless of the financial status and social position you may acquire, you will feel hollow. It is like you volunteer to become an imitation even though you are born as a genuine jewel.

You have all the talents and opportunities to fulfill your plan regardless of how things may appear to be. For example, becoming a CEO of a billion-dollar international corporation is not an impossible dream for the person who has that as a possibility. It may seem ridiculous to other people—the future CEO may be born to a very poor family. And it doesn't mean you can just sit back and the position or the company will fall on your lap. It's only a possibility, and you still need to work toward it. It does, however, mean you have the leadership, business savvy, and what people might call "luck" that make a CEO.

How do you know what is in your plan? Simple. When you are tuned in to who you are, you naturally desire what is in your own plan. After all, it was you who made the plan. You, however, may feel scared about your own dream, and so the whisper of intuition may sound more like "You cannot write," rather than "Writing is my calling," for example. Make no mistake—both are indications of your life plan. If writing is not in your life plan at all, you won't be interested in it; therefore, you won't need to talk yourself out of it.

It is only when you are distracted by what others say and do and thus neglect to pay due attention to yourself that you get confused. In other words, when you disidentify with the ego and realize you are always the soul, you know your plan.

Respecting babies

When we understand we are souls in physical bodies, we have a new respect for babies. Their bodies are weak and undeveloped, but spiritually, they are our equals. Often, babies and small children remember better. Have you ever been surprised by what children have to say about essential issues such as love, compassion, and divinity?

When a soul decides to incarnate, it comes over to this side, usually with a personal spirit guide. The soul follows the parents and eventually starts nurturing the fetus to be born. The soul gets inside the body when the baby is born and takes its first breath. This is when we become fully human, soul with the body.

The soul of the newborn feels quite uncomfortable in the body. They are also surprised that their caretakers don't understand their telepathic communication. So they spend a lot of time sleeping and dreaming of the other side. Eventually, however, they get used to the noisy, flashy world of phenomena and even start enjoying the various stimulations. As their attention shifts from the other side to this side, they forget many of the things they knew. They also figure out that they need to learn the language of their parents. Some babies, however, remember their life on the other side and even their past lives (especially the immediate past life). They attempt to communicate their memories using the few words they have learned, or through doodling and playing.

How will our way of treating babies and children change when we respect them as our spiritual equals? How do you want to be treated when you come back and spend some time as a small child?

Soul age

Some people discuss soul age and seem to assume that an old soul is wise. But how do we count and measure the age of a soul? Do we count how many times the soul has incarnated on Earth? Or do we measure the time since the soul started incarnation? Because the time of each lifetime and in between physical incarnations varies, these two approaches can bring two different results. A soul that has been around for a long time may have gone through only a few incarnations. And what about the souls' experience beyond the Earth plane? Do we count that too? It would be difficult because life on other planets is so different that the comparison wouldn't make much sense.

And as we discussed in Chapter I, time doesn't really exist. It's only a convenient way of organization. So is there a point in discussing soul age? Further, why do we assume old souls are wiser? Within one soul, this may be true, that more experience may have helped the soul to remember the innate wisdom more. But comparisons across the board by age just don't make sense, even when we can count the age, as in biological age. An older person may or may not be wiser than the young.

Like many spiritual issues, "old soul" is just another idea the ego has learned to use to differentiate itself from others. Personally, I am fine that my spirit guides treat me as if I am just a baby. (Well, occasionally, their relentless and unabashed expression of love gets a bit embarrassing and annoying, but I know they mean well.)

Death is neither a punishment nor an honor

Death is another transition in the system of reincarnation. It's a transformation from incarnated form to non-incarnated form. Most souls have done this many times already. You just don't remember.

There is nothing shameful about death. Even when death is caused by a careless accident or an unhealthy lifestyle, death is still not a punishment or failure. How long we live is part of the soul's plan. Typically, we have several options of when and how to exit. In other words, death at a young age does not necessarily mean an unfulfilling, incomplete life.

It's also important not to glorify death of any kind. You don't earn a permanent seat in heaven, even if you die for your country or religion. All deaths work the same way: you go to the other side.

The ego is scared to death about death because the ego ends there. The ego is nothing more than the collection of thoughts and judgments assembled to act like a personality, so while the soul survives death, the ego doesn't. This is why the ego's highest priority is survival. Living for the sake of living, however, doesn't make sense. When we disidentify with the ego, we free ourselves from this paradox and realize the soul's highest priority, which is love.

It is not about wanting to die or rushing to death. It is about accepting death as part of life and incorporating the experience into our overall experience of love.

Predicting one's death

Some souls get to know their upcoming death. This by itself is a good sign, just as any premonition is. Of course, we are not talking about suicide. Suicide is committed by those who think death can end their suffering—it doesn't. All unresolved problems are carried over to the following lifetimes. Awareness of one's pending death happens when the soul is disidentified with the ego and, therefore, understands death as transition. These souls are not scared about the prospect and rather appreciate the time to prepare for it; however, they may find it difficult to discuss this with their loved ones, who are still scared about death.

Swami Vivekananda was probably one such person. He knew he was going to complete his given lifetime in forty years, and sure enough, he made his transition at age thirty-nine. Famous spiritual teachers, however, are not the only ones who can predict their own death. There are probably quite many, and they are not necessarily in poor health. But because few of them discuss the prospect, we don't know that they know their own lifespan.

We typically have several exit points as part of our life plan. For example, someone may plan their first possible exit point around age eighteen. If they decide not to take this early exit, then this person is likely to live on to the next point, say, mid-fifties when they complete their major work. Then, if they again choose to stay around, they might go on for another few decades. This is just one example, and each person's plan is different.

When we are expecting babies, we have no problem thinking and talking about it. We simply prepare for their arrival, both practically and psychologically. When we understand death, we will be able to talk about it with the same loving openness. This will relieve those who know their upcoming departure from carrying the information alone. Thus, the person who is soon leaving as well as their family and friends will be better prepared, making the transition a peaceful experience without regrets.

Crossing over

Some people worry about their loved ones' well-being after death. They are fine. They no longer have a physical body, so they are free of pain, regardless of the way they died. There is no hell and no judges who evaluate us to send us to hell. There is no test to enter heaven, either.

When you die, you, as a soul, leave your physical body. You soon find a special type of spirit guide who is sent to escort you on your way back to the other side. Some people see this escort guide as a bright light. The journey to the other side is sometimes described as crossing a river, sometimes flying through layers in the sky, by those who came back from a near-death experience.

When you get there, after some "welcome home" cheers, you will review your lifetime that just ended. There will be another type of special spirit guides who help you with this, serving as sincere listeners. This review is not judgmental because there is no right or wrong way of living. It's all about how we experienced love, and we review our choices to see if they promoted such experiences. If we ourselves decide we can do things differently next time, we use this insight when we choose the life theme and birth settings for the next incarnation.

(The memory of this review session, however, is probably the foundation of the idea of big judgment. Those who are wrapped in guilt and regret tend to take neutral feedback as criticism or even as an attack.)

There is no rush, however. You can rest on the other side just as long as you like. The length of time in between physical incarnations varies greatly from almost immediate to over a thousand years. Or we can say there is no time and we are experiencing all lifetimes at once—which is true but a harder concept to understand.

Karma is not necessarily bad

Karma is often considered negatively, as in "If you do evil, you will be punished later." Sometimes we even say "karmic debt," and a debt just doesn't sound good. However, karma is really an effective system to experience our purpose of love.

This reality—the giant simulation—has an interesting paradox, or what feels like a paradox. If the purpose of life is to experience love, why are we so different? Wouldn't it be easier if we were more like one another and agreed on many things? It appears as if the world is set up for fighting and for the survival of the meanest and the cruelest.

Not so. If conformity was the point, the Source didn't need to split to begin with. In other words, we are already One in spirit. The point of this simulation in the world of phenomena is to experience love while we appear to be separate. So the paradox is not a paradox at all, but still, many souls get caught up with this. The experience of love, therefore, does not always come easily.

We occasionally make choices that do not lead to love. We often make choices based on the ego. Eventually, such choices prove to be counterproductive to our ultimate purpose. What do we do? Do we have to start the simulation game over from the very beginning? No, there is a much better way. We can just go back to those counterproductive choices and try different options. This is what karma is about.

Karma, which originally meant "action" or "deed" in Sanskrit, is about this system of reviewing our previous deeds and choosing differently. Karma doesn't get back to us unexpectedly. We get back to karma for our highest good. It's like going back to where we bookmarked.

For example, a soul might get so mesmerized with the glittery nature of this perceptual world that it might think love is about getting people to do things for him or her. So this soul (for the sake of this discussion, let's say it is incarnated as a girl) practices how to effectively manipulate men. She polishes her appearance and learns various manipulation techniques. She successfully marries an influential man, and her life is great—she has all the things she can buy and so many people try to please her. For a while she feels loved.

Then she realizes something is wrong. She doesn't feel loved anymore. She doesn't feel love in her, either. But why? Everything went according to her plan of getting love.

Now, if she is wise, she may notice that her idea of love, which has been the foundation of all her endeavors in this lifetime, is wrong. If she is courageous, she can start realizing true love as soon as she notices this, regardless of her age. But what if she doesn't notice? Is she just left behind in misery forever?

No way. At the very least, she can review her life with a spirit guide when she gets to the other side. The spirit guide, being respectful, will not just tell her how she was wrong. It will indicate where the wrong premise may have been so that the soul can plan its next lifetime to explore different options. In this example, she might come back as someone who eventually gets involved with a manipulative partner. When you are in the other person's shoes, you get to see the whole picture and understand better. Through the experience of being manipulated, this soul might realize that love is not about manipulation. Then it can start realizing true love.

The term karma typically indicates receiving the same difficulties that the soul previously imposed on others. It's nothing mysterious—we often experience it in the same lifetime. For example, someone who stole a lover from another may lose that lover in a similar way later. Or someone who got promoted by backstabbing others may lose their position by rootless scandals. It's not a punishment; it's our attempt to remember love, or Oneness.

Can karma be cleared? This question is based on the notion that karma is bad. As we've seen, however, karma is intended to enrich our life experiences in a meaningful way. No one is just left behind in their errors. We are given second, third, or more chances to explore other options. When you remember love in its genuine quality, the karma resolves naturally.

Various patterns of reincarnation

As we reviewed in the beginning of this chapter, souls take various factors into consideration when they plan their rebirth. Choosing to be on the receiving end of the difficulty that it previously imposed on others is one way we explore life. Another common way is to get into a similar situation in order to explore a different path by making different choices.

Throughout life, we make many decisions with our free will. Each decision brings new scenes and another set of available options. This is why people can live different lives even with similar birth settings. Some souls choose to explore the options they missed in previous lifetimes.

For example, let's say you were a middle-class woman in your past life. You decided to marry the man your parents chose for you, a man from the same social and religious group as yourself, even though you were secretly in love with a man from a lower class. You chose to go for parental and social approval rather than being true to your own feelings. This doesn't necessarily mean you made a wrong decision and were unhappy for the rest of your life. But that decision defined your life from there on, and you often wondered what may have happened if you had made a different decision.

In this life, you may be born in surprisingly similar settings —again, a middle-class woman with parents of traditional values. Again, you are secretly attracted to a man that you know your parents would disapprove of. Your parents want you to marry the boy you dated in high school, whose family they know. So what do you do this time? Do you do the same thing again, choosing the option that pleases your parents? Or do you assert yourself this time?

There are various other patterns of reincarnation. None of them are about punishments or rewards. They are just various ways to explore life.

The story of a beautiful woman's reincarnations

Here is a story I wrote to illustrate the process of reincarnation. The description of the other side is simplified for the sake of clarity.

Once upon a time, there lived a very beautiful woman. Not just common-level beautiful—she was breathtaking. Everyone who saw her couldn't help staring at her. They forgot all they were doing and just kept watching her.

She lived in a small village in a remote area. Nonetheless, the rumor of her superior beauty spread all over the country. People traveled a long way just to see her.

Numerous men courted her, sending her letters and gifts. However, she returned all of them because she was in love with a boy in her village. They had known each other since childhood, and all she really wanted was to marry this plain boy and have a loving family.

The king heard of her and came to see her one day. He, too, was impressed with her heavenly beauty and said, "You must come to my castle to be my concubine."

"Oh, Your Majesty," she replied, "that is such an honor. But I already have a fiancé, a man that I promised to marry. Please have mercy and allow me stay here."

"No way," the king replied. "You, who may be more beautiful than the goddesses, marrying a common man? That is so unbecoming of you. You must come with me. Anyone who objects my will must die."

So she had to leave her home village and her love. In the king's castle, she led an exceptionally luxurious life. She was dressed in glossy silk and handmade laces, adorned with gold and precious stones, perfumed with the most expensive flower oils, and many servants cared for her.

When the time of death came, she saw herself leaving her still beautiful body. When she arrived at the other side, she went right to the Reincarnation Service Center and said, "That was not a happy life at all. I want another try, please."

She reincarnated in another country, in another time. The color of her hair and skin were different from the ones she had before, but she was beautiful all the more. As she grew, the rumor of her superior beauty spread all over the country. Newspapers and magazines ran her photos and they sold out. A large talent agency contacted her and persuaded her to appear on TV.

"With your beauty, you can become the most sought-after actress. People will be delighted to see you. You should use your God-given assets to make people happy."

She preferred to have a quiet life with the people she knew, but the agency told her it would be selfish not to share her blessings and asked her to try just once. So she obliged. It didn't end with just one appearance, however. The world went crazy over her beauty and chased her everywhere. Soon she became a famous movie star indeed.

One day, a government agent contacted her.

"We know you travel all over the world as an actress and are invited into the privacy of very important men, the big shots in politics and finances. That is a privilege few can have. We want you to work for our country's secret service."

"What? You want me to work as a spy?" she gasped in surprise.

"Yes, indeed," the agent replied. "Be patriotic and accept this offer, or your family will be imprisoned."

So she had to sleep with men she didn't love in order to steal information and to manipulate those men, while still working as world-famous actress. Her lavish lifestyle became legendary.

When the time of death came, she saw herself leaving her still beautiful body. When she arrived at the other side, she went right to the Reincarnation Service Center and said, "That was not a happy life at all. I want another try, please."

The angel at the counter of the Reincarnation Service Center looked up at her and said, "You are entitled to have another try, or as many tries as you want. But why don't you talk with one of our Guides before you go back to the physical world?"

Before, she was so eager to have another lifetime that she forgot about the guidance service.

So the beautiful woman's soul sat together with one of the Guide spirits. She said, "Last time I was incarnated, I became an actress and then I had to work as a spy. I was rich and famous, people admired me, but for me, that was not a happy life."

"What do you think went wrong?" the Guide asked.

"I lost my freedom when I was forced to work as a spy," she replied.

"I feel sorry for that," the Guide said, "but are you sure you were happy before that? As a famous actress?"

She thought about this for a while and said, "Well, no. I never really felt people understood me when I was an actress. They just saw how beautiful I was and that was it."

"My life before the last one sucked, too," she continued. "I was forced to become the king's concubine. I had everything money could buy, and people treated me with respect, but for me, that was not a happy life."

"What do you think went wrong?" the Guide asked.

"Well, I don't know. Maybe ... I get into troubles because I am too beautiful. Can I be born into a more common-looking body? I don't want to be ugly, but I don't want to attract too much attention," said the beautiful woman.

The Guide went through her file carefully. After a long silence, the Guide said, "No. You are destined to be beautiful. Your colors may change, but you are to be born with superior beauty. You always have been, and always will be."

The woman was shocked.

"Am I ... cursed? Did I do something wrong to be this way?"

"No. It's just one of the parameters that stays the same throughout the many lives you go through. Some souls always have the analytical mind. Some are always talented in music. Likewise, you are always born into beauty. At the same time," the Guide continued, "you want to experience life differently each time, so you can choose different settings, such as the place of birth and social status."

The beautiful woman thought about this carefully. She also noticed the thickness of the file the Guide was holding.

"How many lives have I had? I only remember the last two."

"You've been incarnated hundreds of times on Earth," said the Guide.

"Well, will you tell me about the other past lives I've had? Maybe I can learn from them."

The Guide shook his head and said, "No, the reason you remember only the last two is that those are enough for your reflection. As I said, in all your past lives, you were exceedingly beautiful," the Guide continued. "There have been many tragedies because of this. Many men died fighting to have you. You have been killed many times by women who thought they lost their men because of you. You have also been raped multiple times, sometimes by your brother and other family members. Believe me—it is to your own benefit that you don't remember all your past lives. You would be overwhelmed if you remembered them all."

"How can I change the pattern?" the beautiful woman asked, almost crying.

"Pay attention to what you value in life. And be a bit more assertive about it," the Guide answered.

The beautiful woman's soul came back to the physical world. Needless to say, she was born exceedingly beautiful.

As soon as she was old enough, she asked her parents to send her to a boarding school. The one she chose was in a convent and had a school for the blind on the same grounds. "I want to study nursing and special education," she said, "and become a teacher for the blind."

Her parents were surprised and disappointed. This girl was so beautiful that she could easily become an actress or model or marry a very rich man or ...

But the girl was determined. "If money is the problem, I will apply for a scholarship. I can also work for the blind school as a part-time assistant."

So she went off to the boarding school in the countryside. Although it was not required, she covered her hair like a nun. She worked hard at school and at her work. She enjoyed the quiet life in the country and the small circle of people there.

And when she became a teacher, people finally appreciated her for who she was—even though she was still very beautiful.

Of course, her students never saw her. They simply loved her.

Souls that incarnate together

Souls often incarnate in groups to support one another. They incarnate at about the same time so that they will eventually meet. I call them "soul friends" because the term "soulmate" often implies a one-on-one soul relationship that is predetermined and inflexible. Soul friends, in contrast, are more flexible because friends respect each other's free will while being willing to nurture each other.

Some of your soul friends may be your family members. Some may be your friends and coworkers. Some may be critical people who help you in your toughest challenges. Some are the ones who give you the tough challenges so that you have the opportunity to handle them. The last type may appear to be your nemesis, but they are your soul friends nonetheless.

Soul friends feel familiar even when you first meet them. Spiritually, you know them already because you have spent lifetimes with them before. As the word "friend" suggests, exactly what kind of relationship you may form with your soul friends in this lifetime is up to your free will. You are not obligated to have a certain relationship with your soul friends—you may choose to just say hello and move on this time, and there is no offense. At the same time, it is quite comforting to have some familiar souls around while we tackle this game called life.

I'd like to emphasize that your ideal romantic partner doesn't have to be one of your soul friends. Sure, it's easy to have a relationship with a soul friend—you already know them. Familiarity and comfort, however, are not everything when it comes to relationships. You may be ready to have a relationship with an unfamiliar soul. It may be just the adventure you need.

Benefits of not remembering the past lives

"If we have lived many times already, why don't we remember our past lives? That memory can be a great resource to live better." This is a common question, and the past life information can indeed be helpful if we are free of all emotional hang-ups. Most of us, however, would be overwhelmed if we remembered our past lives. Such memories can also affect our current choices.

For example, imagine you are single and meet someone interesting and attractive. Without the memory, the process of getting to know each other may be time-consuming, but it is an exciting experience. Because you don't remember this person, you can be open to who he or she is now.

But what if you remembered that this person killed you in one of your past lives? This doesn't necessarily mean this is a bad person. While killing another human is not something we want to do, there have been situations in which a good person has killed fellow humans, such as in wars or in fights that got out of control. This soul may be coming to you in this lifetime to make amends. Yet such a memory can leave you feeling bitter and confused.

So, unless you are completely open to love and ready to accept everything as it has been, the temporary amnesia works for you. And for those who are ready to receive even the seemingly bad news, the information is stored in the Akashic Records, which are accessible by everyone.

The end of reincarnation

If the merit of forgetting past lives is to open up to love experiences with freshness and spontaneity, and the reason for our death is our emotional overload and resulting physical deterioration, then we will forgo such amnesia and even death when we fully accept our innate loving nature. This can happen in two phases. First, we will retain our awareness through the cycles of reincarnation. Then, physical death will be postponed indefinitely because it becomes unnecessary. This is what the end of reincarnation means.

It seems we leave the majority of our past life memory when we leave the other side to be reborn. Then we forget about the other side as we get used to the life in this world as infants. Although it may appear to be otherwise, death does not disrupt our awareness—as we reviewed, souls remember the life that just ended.

Can we wholeheartedly love and accept our former enemies, which means they are not enemies to begin with? So maybe a better question is: Can we just love everyone, everything, and every event for what they are? Can we live with zero resentment, zero doubt, and zero intolerance? When we realize love in this genuine state, we feel as if we can keep living for good, and we will.

Taoists have legends of immortal masters. The Bible tells us about the resurrection of Jesus. Jesus' death is often explained as the compensation for our sins, but as we reviewed in Chapter I, there is no original sin. Our exercise of free will is precisely what is expected of us and needs no compensation. The misunderstanding is due to the fear of death. If you think death is the ultimate bad experience, someone who dies for no fault of their own is a hero or a victim, or both.

Jesus chose to die so that he could show us the possibility of resurrection. If he could walk on water, he could surely walk away from the cross or avoid getting caught to begin with. For him, however, healing the sick and turning water to wine were minor miracles. Rather than doing more of such minor miracles, he chose to show us the big miracle, the possibility to defy death as we know it. In order to do that, he first had to die in public—which was, apparently, scary even for him.

Most people who seek the end of reincarnation, however, are in a completely different mindset. They hate life and don't want it ever again. This indicates that they are identifying with the ego. The soul knows only to love. So when they die and, therefore, their ego ceases to exist, they, as the soul, realize they didn't fulfill what they came to this world for: to experience love. Therefore, they reincarnate.

We are never tired of life. But we may grow tired of our idea of life. Life itself is ever fresh and sweet. But we tend to zoom in to the few things we don't find favorable—due to the shortsightedness of the ego—and build ideas about life based on this distorted view. Then we agonize over this idea we made and find more reasons to support the idea. This way of living only makes reincarnation more necessary.

The true end of reincarnation comes with enlightenment, which is just one way to say disidentification with the ego. It is not about an end, but about the beginning of a new way of life, life that doesn't require renewal through death and rebirth. Life that is about genuine love, filled with unwavering joy.

PRACTICING LOVE

We are all visitors to this time, this place.
We are just passing through.
Our purpose here is to observe,
to learn, to grow, to love ...
and then we return home.
— Australian Aboriginal proverb

Remembering love

Few words have been misunderstood more than "love," perhaps with the exception of "God" (which is ultimately the same, as we have seen). Most of us refer to a kind of business transaction with this four-letter word. This is why some people say, "Love only those who love you back," which makes perfect sense if love was meant to be something that we provide in order to be paid back, as in business trades. Others say, "Don't love too much, you might get hurt." Again, if it were a business, we would need to watch the balance carefully so that we wouldn't go broke. That's just healthy business sense. Some even see love as an investment and expect to get more than they put in. They would say, "Love is not enough," when their expectations to get more are not fulfilled.

Love has been confused with infatuation and attachment. So when we mean the kind of love we have been discussing in this book, we may have to add clarifying words and say something like "unconditional love" or use less tainted words like "compassion."

None of these are love's fault, however. Love has never changed. Deep inside, we all know true love. We just need to remember this love, and we can do so when we disidentify with the ego. As long as you think you are the mental image you think you are, you only crave love and cannot experience love, no matter who or what the object of your love may be.

Love is the realization that we are all interconnected and part of the whole. We all come from the Source, and each one of us is an essential part of the universe. We are like parts of one body. The kidney is just as important as the heart. The heart does not look down on the kidney because it deals with urine, but loves the kidney for its uniqueness. The heart loves every organ and tissue of the body for what they are, and so does every part of the body for every other part of the body. The kidney does not need to be more like the heart—it is great as it is, and so is every organ and every tissue of the body. Together, they make the whole, a single body, that is greater than the sum of its parts. So do we. Everyone and everything in the universe is connected. This realization of Oneness is the true essence of love.

There is nothing manipulative about true love, and therefore, true love may appear detached. Love says: "I see how I am. I see how you are. I love and accept you as you are, as I love and accept myself as I am. You don't need to change anything about you unless you yourself choose to. Nor do I change for you." And it is this gentle acceptance that harmonizes us all.

Love allows freedom for the beloved, even the freedom to leave. It surely grants the freedom to make mistakes, or to make decisions that bring out challenging situations. Challenges are part of this life simulation game after all. Love doesn't judge the person by their choices and deeds. Love says: "I trust and respect that you will eventually find your path on your own, whatever it may be. You don't need to agree with me—I love your 'yes' and I love your 'no.' I may get upset at you, but I still love you. You use your free will to do what you believe to be right. You live your life, with your choices and their results. It's just an additional honor and fun to have you in my life while we both enjoy it."

Love cannot be defined

Discussing love is innately difficult because love is far bigger than any definition or description. Love nurtures. Love also challenges. Love is peaceful. Love is courageous. Love is light-hearted. Love is wise. Love is extraordinary and yet every-where. Love is you. Love is me. Love is ... infinite. Love just is.

This is why I had to use the analogy of the body to describe what love is like rather than defining what love is. The good news is we don't need to learn love from scratch. We already know love deep within; we need only to remember it. Unlearning the businesslike fake love is part of this remembering.

Even a baby knows love. In fact, babies are great reminders of love because they have not learned fake love yet. When they cry, they are simply expressing their needs. They know their needs are important, so they are not shy about expressing them. Please note that they don't cry to manipulate. They don't operate in the line of "You didn't feed me quickly enough yesterday, so I am going to punish you by crying louder today." They have preferences, as part of their unique character, but they don't judge. A baby might like one of its caretakers more than others, but it is only their preference, not the result of their judgment. When they have slept enough and been fed enough, they smile at everyone. They don't smile because you've done something for them—they smile even at the casual passersby. They also love life—they even accept the painful experiences of learning to walk. Anyone who has watched babies grow is amazed at how eager they are to try new things, regardless of the numerous failures such exploration involves.

Love is like the air. It is not about a special person or a special day. We are in love all the time, whether we are aware of it or not. Love is the default and non-love is the illusionary irregularity, similar to holding our breath. We can learn how to express love in ways others can understand, but love itself cannot be taught or learned, nor does it need to be.

Truthfully, it is even more than that. Love is not only around us, but we are made of love. And this is why we cannot define love. As we have seen in Chapter II, we cannot define the "I." Every definition defies the truth and leads to the limited idea of self. Likewise, every definition of love defies the truth. I can only know I am here and I am love.

We, as physical beings, pass, but love is eternal. We, as spiritual beings, are the love itself. We are here in the world of phenomena to explore the endless manifestations of one love.

The universe whispers, "I love you"

The universe or the Source or God is always talking to us. It is in a language of energy, so it leaves some room for interpretation. I tend to hear its gentle, nurturing quality. To me, it sounds like "I love you." The "I" and "you" are very weak, and I understand they are added to make sense in human language; in truth, there is no "I" or "you." There is only love.

And it goes on continuously like the ocean's murmur, "I love you ... I love you ... I love you ...." Perhaps this is why so many people don't notice it; the message is so constant that it becomes a background sound.

The love and its message are always there. We live in infinite love. It's the mother of all love. Every love we experience is a variation of this big love. Next time when you are in nature, maybe when you can look up at the stars, please take time to be silent and "listen." You might also hear the message spontaneously in your most ordinary moment.

Love and empowerment

A common misunderstanding about love is that love and power are incompatible. This misunderstanding is based not only on the misbelief of love but also on the misbelief of power. We often think of power as an external, manipulative force. Political powers, financial powers, and even religious powers have been controlling and limiting our lives throughout history. Because of this, many of us have developed resentment against power. On the personal level, power is often associated with money and sex, two topics we have strong, mixed feelings about.

Power, however, is innate within each of us. We are endorsed with natural power to come into existence and to live our lives in this physical world. Getting incarnated takes a miraculous amount of power and so does growing up and living. This vital power, or energy, comes directly from the Source. By default, we receive this energy on an ongoing basis—no special efforts are required for this. The universal Source energy feeds and supports us. The primary nature of this Source energy is love, so love and this power are one and the same. It is the one true power in the universe, and this power eventually wins over all fake powers. Gandhi is an example of those who knew this truth. Anyone who has deeply loved also knows how empowering love can be.

It is important to note that we tend to be drawn to false power when we forget our innate power and feel powerless. People who manipulate others in the name of love—possibly to the level of abuse—are well liked by those who don't realize their own inner love and power. The key to releasing oneself from such consuming relationships, then, is within ourselves.

Love and wisdom

True love is also wise and insightful because the Source energy, which is the essence of love, is intelligent. Wisdom is far more than the accumulation of knowledge. Knowledge can be gained and memorized quite mechanically, but it is love that gives meaning to knowledge. The energy of love also connects us to the pool of knowledge and wisdom that is not accessible by our conventional approach.

"Love is blind," is the sentiment of the ego. The ego thinks it is smart and rejects ideas that do not fit with its survival strategies. The ego's smartness, however, is limited because the ego itself is limited in its perception and understanding. The ego doesn't understand love, which values the connection more than the individual. So love threatens the very operating system of the ego, as we reviewed in Chapter II. In doing so, love leads us to the eternal wisdom of the soul.

Love's wisdom may feel counter to what we usually consider as wisdom. Love drives us to do silly things, such as driving hundreds of miles just to see the person we love and doing things for the sheer joy of seeing their delight. In truth, we are going beyond the boundary of self through such actions. We are opening up to the wisdom that is far bigger than conventional wisdom. So be okay with the seeming silliness of love, and even when the loving relationship ends, do not go back to the bitterness of the ego, saying, "That was such a waste."

Love, wisdom, and power are the three aspects of the Source energy. Everyone has all the love, wisdom, and power within oneself. The love you receive is only the reflection of your own love. The wisdom you find is not learned but remembered. The power is always within, waiting to be exercised.

Self-love as the foundation of love

Love takes us beyond the confines of the self, yet the mystery is that self-love is the foundation of all love. Self-denial and sacrifice are not love and non-love never leads to love. In other words, when you unconditionally and totally love yourself, you just started to love the whole of humanity and beyond because we are all One.

The misunderstanding that self-love conflicts with love for others is based on the idea of love as a limited resource, like other resources in this physical world. If it is a limited resource, we need to figure out how to distribute it fairly, and wanting more than one's share can be considered greedy. Love, however, is spiritual and can expand infinitely. The more you love, the more love you have, and there is no end. There is no need to be frugal about love, nor to try to figure out if it should be given to oneself or to others.

The misunderstanding about self-love is also due to the ego's attempt to get what it wants in the name of love. The ego doesn't really understand love. Instead, it uses the word "love" as a nice negotiation tool, as in "If you love me, you would ...." The idea of self-love is used in this way as well, as justification for doing what the ego does: "I put myself over others because I love myself." This is not about real self-love at all.

Unfortunately, the misbelief that love is about self-denial has been handed down for a long time, and we tend to confuse self-love with selfishness and arrogance. This has further reinforced the misunderstanding as people fear to be viewed as such a self-centered person.

Loving others while not loving oneself is like cooking for others while starving oneself. There is plenty of food. What is the point of not serving yourself? You probably want to taste it even before you serve it to others. And if you keep starving yourself, eventually, the sense of hunger and resentment will take the better part of you. You will also have less energy to cook for others, which is counterproductive. The people around you surely don't want this to happen to you.

You might think this would work if they feed you with love in return. But there is undeniable awkwardness in this picture: If you are well enough to cook, why can't you feed yourself? Two or more able individuals saying, "I take care of you, you take care of me," is called codependency. It is a self-defeating expectation because, when you love someone with the expectation to be loved back, it's not love anymore—it's manipulation. Codependency, or people-pleasing, may appear similar to love and kindness, but it is ego-based and therefore not love.

We have a tendency to make hasty judgments based on appearances and other superficial impressions. Our challenge is to see through such illusions and live by truth, and the most essential truth is that love is within. In order to truly love, we must remember this innate love and expand the realization.

Love for who you are

Self-love is also a perfect place to practice the unconditionality of love. You know yourself well, with all the imperfections and what you consider to be unlovely qualities. Can you still love yourself as you are? If not, how can you love someone as they are? Double standards never work. If you are judgmental toward yourself, then you are judgmental toward others, whether you voice it or not.

Love is about accepting who the person is. It doesn't compare them to the hypothetical ideal. Therefore, true love doesn't ask the person to change or interfere with their changes. If we love on the condition that the person will change to our preference, it is not love but manipulation. Manipulation simply doesn't feel good, no matter how well it is disguised. By practicing self-love and being both the giver and receiver of your own love, you can remember how true love feels, free of any stickiness of manipulation.

Self-love, then, is not about self-esteem. Self-esteem can be a healthy concept if it means respect for who you are, the individual you that is uniquely twisted. However, because we usually identify with the ego, which is about comparison and judgment, self-esteem implies we need to be in a respectable condition, that we need to deserve our own respect. This leads to the idea that we must achieve something noteworthy or possess something valuable. Therefore, the attempt to have self-esteem usually leaves us feeling as if we are not enough. Ironically, self-esteem typically leads us away from self-love.

Each of us is unique, and our uniqueness is the perfect contribution to the whole. This uniqueness of each soul—your personality—doesn't change, so why don't we choose to love it rather than resenting it? Love, love, and love yourself with all your heart, like your life depends on it, like the whole universe depends on it, because it does. Love yourself just the way you are until, when you look in the mirror, you see divinity in your own eyes.

Embracing solitude

In order to love freely and unconditionally, we first need to embrace solitude. If you need someone with you in order to feel good, you will have to manipulate that person to be with you. Such manipulation is quite common. If, for example, you smile at someone not because you are happy or because you bless them but because you want them to think of you favorably, you are manipulating. It's the same with any gift, such as kindness, together-time, and affection. In order for these gifts to be true gifts of love, we need to give them away with no expectation of getting something back. In other words, we need to be okay to end up in solitude.

Love doesn't start when you meet someone. Love starts in solitude. Many people, however, are silently afraid of facing themselves. They make themselves extremely busy with various chores so that they don't have to consciously face themselves. When you live this way, however, what you see in yourself is the person who is afraid of their own reflection. Then you judge this fearful figure as stupid and cowardly. In effect, you further reinforce your identification with the ego, and your fear grows. It's a vicious cycle, and the way out is by choosing to take time for yourself and remembering to love who you are.

Take plenty of time to be by yourself and to get to know yourself. Embracing solitude means more than simply being alone, just as intimacy is more than proximity. It's about loving and enjoying oneself. Review what you consider to be defective about yourself and discover how it can work for you. (It probably has already.) A characteristic is a characteristic, neither good nor bad. Our strengths are the flip side of our weaknesses, and vice versa. We notice this truth when we accept ourselves as we are.

Do the things you like to do. Try new things as well. Get familiar with what pure enjoyment feels like. Get to know your fears and angers as well. Own all your feelings and be familiar with what triggers them in you. Take good care of your body and mind. It's hard to enjoy anything while you are uptight.

Please note that this is not about analyzing oneself. Often, the ego walks right in and starts giving explanations and excuses for who you are. Like other things the ego says, the explanation only sounds interesting but is not true. Here is the difference: When you analyze yourself, you put yourself in a category. Then you think the label of that category describes you or you argue against it. When you get to know yourself as you are, you see the actual you, the you who cannot be categorized and labeled because you are unique and unprecedented. You see yourself fresh and vivid.

When you practice solitude, you will notice something quite wonderful: You are never really alone. In you and through you, the Source energy is always flowing. You are always connected to everything and everyone with this invisible energy. The comfort and guidance you seek are already within, and you can feel them in solitude.

Alone time also reminds you of the life plan you made prior to birth and helps you to choose the path that is most appropriate for yourself. Taking time for yourself, therefore, is one of the most effective ways to use time.

Being open and vulnerable

Being willing to be open and vulnerable is the prerequisite of love. The energy of love can flow in only as much as your heart is open. Love is always present, but you need to choose love and let it come in. When you open your heart, you also let your own love flow out freely. This means letting others see who you are, which feels vulnerable.

If love is power, why do we feel vulnerable in love? This question is based on a misunderstanding of power and vulnerability. Do we want to be like robots, with our sensitivity turned off, and therefore being able to do even cruel things? Such so-called power has nothing to do with the power of the Source energy and love. Our very human power comes from daring to be vulnerable when we can choose to shut down and choosing courage while feeling vulnerable. So please familiarize yourself with the sense of vulnerability. Once you do, you'll find vulnerability is delightfully beautiful, like tender petals opening up and being seen.

We simply cannot use our past hurts as an excuse to stay behind the closed door of our own heart. That leads only to more pain, this time due to suffocation. Besides, past hurt is no prediction that the same damage will happen again. We need to show up for our own life, with courage to love.

This, however, doesn't mean you must expose yourself. It's wonderful when we openly and freely give ourselves; when we smile, hug, kiss and make love just because. Please note that this freedom also grants us the freedom to say no. We don't even need to explain the no, just as we don't need to explain the yes.

Disagreements in love

One of the major questions about love is, "When we love a person unconditionally, do we have to love all their choices? What if their choice is against my morals? Against their own best interest? Against my self-love?"

Love is not about becoming like twins. Love is about loving the person as they are, including their unique differences. Sure, things are easier when we agree, but disagreement doesn't mean the lack of love. Even when you don't agree or support the decision your loved one makes, you can still love that person. Love their yes and love their no; whether you choose to play along with each of their choice is up to you.

Part of the confusion comes from the word "unconditional." We add this clarifying word to distinguish love from business-like fake love; unconditional love means love with no judgment, as conditions are based on judgments. However, for the ego, which doesn't understand love and only uses the idea as negotiation tool, the word "unconditional" is a way to strengthen the negotiation. So some people use the idea to justify whatever they fancy to do and manipulate others, as in "If you love me unconditionally, you will stay with me no matter what I do." Then others internalize this idea and feel as if they should agree with everything their loved one says.

While love allows the freedom of disagreement, we don't want to jump to judgment. So a wise approach you can take when you are unsure of your loved one's choices is to listen to them wholeheartedly.

Listen with the sincere intention to understand what they are going through and how they are feeling. No interruption. No agenda to change their choices. No judgment on their choices. Just listen and listen through.

Most people would find this very hard to do because we are used to listening for the sake of inserting our opinions—our ego's opinions mostly. For example, we don't really know what is in their or our own best interest—we just think we do. We hardly listen because we are busy thinking what we will say when there is any pause. We criticize. We advise. We share our experiences that we believe to be similar to theirs, with the intent to change their mind. We persuade. We coax. We might even bribe. We really need to practice the art of listening wholeheartedly, which is, by itself, an act of love.

Listening with the full intention to understand their choice, without the intention to change them, is very loving—so loving that it may change their choice. Or maybe not. Sometimes, the most loving thing we can do is to let our loved ones figure out their lives on their own, through trials and errors. (When you are dealing with children, you may need to modify this approach because children do need some guidance and protection. Exactly how much modification is appropriate depends on their age, maturity, and so on.)

Why we are attracted to certain souls

Take a moment and think of the people you care about—your family members, your significant other, your friends—and think why you like them. Do you like them because they have achieved perfection? Are you attracted to the kind of excellence that can be evaluated and proven?

No, the attraction is more about how you feel when you are with them. When you like your friend for his great sense of humor, for example, it means you like the lightheartedness you feel when you are with him. So you share laughter, and this experience builds your history of friendship. It's not about your friend being a great comedian that the world would acknowledge. Likewise, when you like someone because she is wise, it means you like the brilliant feeling she brings forth in you. Exactly how wise she is in comparison to others is not the point. When you like someone because she is beautiful, it means you like the way she looks and how you feel seeing her. She probably didn't have to win the beauty contest.

What is happening is resonance. We sense in others what is in ourselves. If you are not witty at all and you don't value a sense of humor, you won't find your funny friend to be a likable person. You might think you like someone because they have something you don't possess, but this is a short-sighted understanding. At the very least, you have the seed for that quality, and that is the very reason you value people who already exhibit it.

We are attracted to the people who serve as a reminder of our own inner greatness by first showing that great quality. This means the more you love yourself and value your own characteristics, the more you love others. So all relationships reflect your own self-love, and in turn, relationships nurture further self-love.

By the same token, if you dislike certain qualities in yourself, you will dislike people who exhibit the same qualities. If you are working hard to fix that aspect of yourself, you will feel judgmental toward people who have the same tendency and don't appear to be fixing them. If you are trying to ignore that quality in yourself, you will be upset at people who shamelessly exhibit it. Again, it is not really about them but about how you feel about yourself.

We project our own self-love or the lack thereof on others and believe it is about them. Because the ego shifts its attention frequently and unexpectedly, like a small child does, you might see what you like about yourself in a person, fall madly in love with him or her, then one day, start seeing what you don't like about yourself in the same person. It might feel like that person has changed, or started to reveal the qualities that they have been hiding. But no—it's really about the way you see them, and until you notice this, the pattern will continue.

The way you see people and the world tells you how you really feel about yourself. Because we see in others what we see in ourselves, a self-loving soul finds more and more reason to love in others. Self-love and love for others don't conflict but grow together. If, on the other hand, you find faults in so many people, it's time to embrace solitude and the way you are. There's no need to be judgmental about this—that is not a loving approach.

In other words, don't just surround yourself with agreeable people. Allow those who irritate you to come to you because they are coming to show you where you need more self-love. And you will find that, when you appreciate them this way, those who rub against you come only when you need the reminders. We are living in the simulation, remember?

The meaning of relationships

The true meaning of relationships, then, is in recognizing oneself through another person and deepening that understanding over a period of time. The love starts within oneself, gets reflected on another soul, and comes back.

Many people, however, skip the first step and start looking for a partner right away. They think of relationships as the only way to taste the joy of love and as the safe haven in a potentially unkind and dangerous world. They hold their breath for the day they find the ideal relationship, and they look for it everywhere outside themselves. Just finding someone to love, however, is not enough. They hold on to the relationship tight, which is a sure way to suffocate it, and when it falls short of their expectations, they blame their partner. Surely, they think, there must be a better partner ....

This is like running around blindfolded. You will surely get hurt this way. Why not take the blindfold off and look at yourself and your surroundings. Then you see all the love in the universe is flowing through you. This is already great, but you might find a variation of fun when you shine your love on another being and see the beautiful reflection. There is a reason why we look into the eyes of our beloved.

We are essentially One, but we, as the Source, split so that we can play this game of feeling separate and therefore finding one another. It's a sophisticated variation of hide-and-seek. In a sense, we have relationships with everyone and everything in the universe. We see ourselves in everyone and everything. Whether we like what we see depends on how we feel about ourselves, not on how they are.

While we are in relationships with everyone, however, there is a point in developing close relationships with a limited number of souls; it deepens our understanding of ourselves. Plus, it is a delicious experience.

Soulmate myth

Perhaps it is clear by now that, if you are seeking that one special soul, a soulmate, you are missing great opportunities. Because most of us have been incarnated many times already, there are indeed souls that are familiar to you. A group of souls, that I call "soul friends" (Chapter III), have been incarnated together repeatedly, so they feel especially familiar. This, however, does not mean you should have a romantic relationship with one of them. It also doesn't mean a relationship with one of them would be guaranteed to be problem-free and long-lasting.

If you are seeking a soulmate, ask yourself why. Is it because you want to have a deep, meaningful relationship? That's great. The opportunities are many. Or is it because you think that, once you find your soulmate, everything will be great and you will be happy ever after? Such expectations are usually based on past hurt and resentment. Do you think the reason your past relationship failed is that you were with the wrong person? Are you afraid of getting into a relationship with another wrong person, and therefore holding your breath for the wonderful soulmate? Such fear-based expectation doesn't work because you see only the reflection of your own fear in others.

It is also essential to understand that the value of a relationship cannot be measured by its length. A great relationship that leads to a deep realization of love may or may not last for the rest of your life.

Another problem with the idea of soulmate is that it undermines our free will. There is no one that you must have a relationship with because it is meant to be. Nobody can or should pursue you because they believe you are their soulmate. A good relationship is based on the free will of both parties, not a soulmate contract or any other binding promises. The more freedom you allow in a relationship, the more meaningful it will be.

A romantic relationship is one of the ways we experience love in this physical world. Let it be free because that is how love is.

Our sexuality is a blessing

Many religions have condemned sexuality. They teach that flesh is inferior to spirit. When we understand how we started this reality, however, we understand that both our spirit and flesh are essential, as both our Oneness and individuality are essential. They are interrelated, and condemning one over the other would only end in oxymoron. The very physical act of sex can bring this realization. When we feel the best orgasm, it is not just physical but far more than that—we realize, beyond logic, we are more than the body alone.

And this is precisely what organized religions have feared. If people freely enjoyed full orgasms, they would know they can access spiritual truth without going through religious organizations. So they have loaded sex with guilt in their attempts to limit the level of orgasm. It has been a political issue, and controlling sex brought additional political control, such as population control and male dominance over females.

Male bashing is pointless when we know we have incarnated as both male and female and will continue to do so. The discussion of gender needs to be based on this understanding that we can exist both as male and female, and to be factual rather than emotional. When I say "male dominance over females," I am simply pointing out the historical fact that has existed over the last few thousand years, which I have been a part of on both sides.

As souls, we have both male and female aspects. As physically incarnated beings, we are either a man or a woman, and this sexuality is a blessing. Sometimes it is our last resort. We are here to experience love in its many beautiful variations, but occasionally we get so tired that we lose interest in more tender forms of love. Even then, sexual energy can guide us to love, which can restore our overall energy.

Let's celebrate sexuality while we are physical. It's not about promiscuity—although that is an option that can be chosen freely. The concept of promiscuity makes sense only in contrast to chastity and monogamy. Why, we can even celebrate sexuality while having no sexual contact at all. It's about owning one's sexuality and trusting passion and pleasure.

Gratitude, or not taking anything for granted

Gratitude is acknowledging your love and appreciation. Don't be stingy with gratitude—that only limits your awareness of love. Express gratitude for everything, everyone, and every event. This includes what you consider to be bad or negative because, for one, you don't really know if something is bad and also because a negative can work as a reminder of the positive.

A great way to practice this big realization of gratitude is the gratitude journal. Just write down what you are grateful for. In the beginning, you would probably write something that is easy to be grateful for, such as your family and friends, your health, things you find to be enjoyable like good meals and flowers, and so on. See if you can add new things you are grateful for each day. You will soon see how great it is to have a roof over your head and some money in the bank. Even if your health is not ideal, you can be grateful for the parts of the body that are free of pain; then be grateful for the parts that are hurting but are still working. Try not to miss the small things to be grateful for, such as your neighbor who greets you with a smile, the little kindness from a store clerk, or the song you happened to hear that lifted your mood. Nothing is too petty to be grateful for.

Pay attention to details so that your gratitude is not just a nice idea but something with real feeling. For example, if, in the beginning, you just wrote that you are grateful for having your children, see if you can write some of the things about them that delight you, such as the way they smile or the way their hugs feel. If you think you should be grateful for your job, see if you can write some of the aspects of your job that you actually appreciate, for example, the learning opportunities it provides and the people you have had the honor to meet through the job.

There are always many, many things to be grateful for. For fun, pick several things that you happen to notice around you, and see if you can feel grateful for them. You don't need to own the things, by the way—just their presence is sufficient to be grateful for. What would life be like without seeing butterflies once in a while?

But what about the disagreeable people in your life? Can you be grateful for them? This is a great challenge, so take your time. See if there is something about them, however small, that you can be grateful for. If not, see if you can consider them as disguised teachers—someone who is showing you important values, such as compassion and tolerance, by displaying what life would be like when you don't embrace them. They are playing that role so that you don't have to. Isn't this something to be grateful for?

Eventually, you will realize that everything happens for you. Even the things that seem to be no good happen for us so that we can remember our innate love and power. We chose them according to our life plan that we made prior to birth, so do not let your ego judge them. Embrace them with gratitude, and you will move through the experience with relative ease.

This big gratitude for everything is not the same as the conceptual gratitude you think you should be feeling. You will actually feel grateful for everyone in your life for being the precious unique person they are. You will feel grateful for everything that is happening to you because, in the big scheme that you may not be ready to understand yet, everything is happening for you.

Living in constant love and gratitude is the essence of spirituality. When you are in constant love and gratitude, you do not need any dogma. You see divinity in yourself and in everyone, everything.

The story of a rich man, a king, a guru and a woman

While we already know love as spirit, practicing love in this dazzling world of phenomena is quite challenging. And that's the whole point of this simulation. So there's no need to feel bad if your love is not free of manipulation yet. You are on the track, and your great experience of love may be closer than you think.

Ultimately, when you are so purely love, people who come close to you will forget the bitterness and resentment they may have been carrying around. Love has a cleansing property that renews our existence.

In order to have a clear image of a person with such love, I wrote a short story, a modern-day parable. I'd like to wrap up this chapter with this story.

Once upon a time, there lived a woman who was quite nondescript. Her name was ... well, no one really knew, something that starts with A, like Ada or Alisha. Let's call her Ada for now.

She lived in a little cottage at the edge of a small town. There was a big apple tree in front of the house, and people occasionally saw her talking with someone under that tree. And then at other times, people saw her there sitting alone.

A very rich man heard about Ada and got curious. So he visited her and said, "Hey, Ada, I heard about you. You seem interesting. What would you say if I invite you over to my grand resort so we can talk a bit? I mean, I'm really busy, so I will be in and out, but you can enjoy expensive meals, a spa massage, or whatever you like when I'm out. Nice, huh?"

Ada replied, "Thank you. That sounds fantastic. But we can just talk under that tree now. Like, how we are already talking."

So they settled in the chairs under the tree.

The rich man said, "I am really, really rich. There is nothing I cannot buy in this world. And did you know pretty much everything is for sale, perhaps except the sun and the stars?"

Ada replied, "It's great you are happy with what you have. And true, we share the sun and the stars."

The rich man felt puzzled because Ada wasn't impressed with his astronomical fortune. Yet she felt warm, and sitting under the tree was pleasant, so he continued.

"I wasn't born rich. In fact, I was born to a very poor family. When I was a young boy, there were many things I couldn't have because my parents couldn't afford them. So I was determined to get rich. I worked hard, I invested the money I made, I took chances. I am a self-made man, and I am proud I have made a lot of money."

Ada replied, "Yes, I see the diligence in you."

Now the rich man was frustrated. The people he had met so far tried hard to please him. But Ada hadn't changed her attitude at all since he entered her little cottage. He could sense she was the same way before he came, and she would be the same way after he left.

"Ada, I can buy you anything. Tell me what you want."

Ada replied, "Thank you. But I am okay as I am."

The rich man felt a release in him that he never felt before. He didn't know what to do anymore, so he decided to leave.

"I must go now. May I visit you again?"

"Sure," Ada replied.

The ruling king of the country heard about Ada and got curious. So he visited her and said, "I am the powerful king of this country, and because this is the biggest country in the world, I practically rule over the whole world. Of course you know me, Ada, don't you?"

Ada seldom read the news, but she thought she had heard about him. So she gently smiled and kept listening.

The king said, "You seem interesting. What would you say if I make you my advisor? This way, you can control the world in the way you like. And I can talk with you anytime."

Ada replied, "I appreciate your offer, but we can just talk under that tree now. Like, how we are already talking."

So they settled in the chairs under the tree.

The king said, "I can order anyone to do anything. You, Ada, better do what I tell you to do, or I can torture and kill you. See all the men over there waiting for my command?"

Ada replied, "It's great you are happy with what you can do. I am here now, and true, I don't know where I'd be the next moment."

The king felt agitated because he was used to people immediately obeying him. He looked at Ada sternly for a while.

Then he said, "I am not a bad, cruel person. Politics takes a huge toll on me because I don't know whom to trust. Even my brother or wife may betray me—there have been such cases in history. I try to do the right things, but there are always people who want this, and other people who want different things. I'm stressed because I cannot make everyone happy."

Ada replied, "Yes, I see the generosity in you."

The king felt his heart soften, and he almost cried. However, he didn't like such a weak feeling, so he said, "Ada, I can do anything for you. If the position of my advisor is not what you want, tell me what you do want."

Ada replied, "Thank you. But I am okay as I am."

The king felt a release in him that he never felt before. He didn't know what to do anymore, so he decided to leave.

"I must go now. May I visit you again?"

"Sure," Ada replied.

A guru heard about Ada and got curious. So he visited her and said, "Ada, I have lived one thousand years and learned how to communicate with God and the angels. I can use magic to make anything happen. Why don't you come to my secret place so that we can talk and change the world with my magic?"

Ada replied, "Thank you. That sounds interesting. But we can just talk under that tree now. Like, how we are already talking."

So they settled in the chairs under the tree.

The guru said, "Maybe you didn't fully understand my supernatural power. Do you have any health problems? I can heal you. I can make you a young, beautiful woman. I can give you talents to achieve anything. I can even show you how to get out of your body and fly."

Ada replied, "Why do I want these things? I am fine with who I am."

The guru was surprised because he had seen millions of men and women coming to him to have their wishes granted. He believed everyone had wishes.

The guru changed his tone of voice and said, "I can also send you to hell so you forever suffer there."

To that, Ada replied, "I know I am here. You cannot trick me to go to a place that does not exist."

The guru's face became red with anger. Then he became pale with fear. He said, "Forgive me. I am not a crazy, manipulative person. I started studying magic because I thought it would save many people's lives."

Ada replied, "Yes, I see the sincerity in you."

The guru felt a release in him that he never felt before. He didn't know what to do anymore, so he decided to leave.

"I must go now. May I visit you again?"

"Sure," Ada replied.

Eventually, death came to all.

In his death bed, the rich man recalled his life. It was a dramatic life, starting from a humble birth, rising to the beautiful life of luxury. He recalled the people he met in his life. His fellow business owners, various celebs ... and then he remembered the woman he once talked to. He could not remember her name or her face, but he remembered the warm, relaxed feeling he felt when he was with her.

"She knew me," he thought. And that brought some comfort.

In his death bed, the king recalled his life. It was a dignified life, a life of honor and high order. He recalled the people he met in his life. His royal family members, brilliant and dedicated men and women who served his country under his name ... and then he remembered the woman he once talked to. He could not remember her name or her face, but he remembered the warm, relaxed feeling he felt when he was with her.

"She knew me," he thought. And that brought some comfort.

The guru was practically immortal, but the day came when he grew tired of living in this physical world, so he decided to leave. He recalled his long, mysterious life. He recalled the people he met in his life ... and the spirits he encountered in other dimensions ... and then he remembered the woman he once talked to. He could not remember her name or her face, but he remembered the catalysis he felt in himself when he talked with her.

No one knows when and where Ada passed away.

THE INFINITE
WISDOM WITHIN

There is a voice that doesn't use words.
Listen.
— Rumi

Intuition as a navigation system

Wisdom starts in humility. If I assume I already know the answer, I will not be open to new possibilities, and this limits my wisdom. Besides, the very assumption that I already know the answer is quite immature.

The ego likes to think it knows all the answers. It does not. It has only piles of knowledge and makes judgments based on that knowledge. Its judgment is always based on outdated material. While we don't need to hate the ego, we do need to humbly leave the ego to access bigger wisdom.

Wisdom is not in authorities and their books, either. Even with good intentions, people can offer only their views and understandings, and in order for me to utilize such external information, I need to access the wisdom within.

Under the loud dictation of the ego, there is a "voice" or direct knowing. As souls, we know our life plan. Deep within, we know how this giant life simulation game works. We also share all the knowledge of everyone and everything in the Akashic Records. This knowing, or the way to access this knowing, is called intuition. Intuition is the navigation system in this simulation game. In order to fully practice love and realize our Oneness, it is essential to be aware of this inner wisdom.

Our brain is like a computer. It can work as a stand-alone computer, processing data and thoughts, and it can also work as a network computer that is connected to the vast collective wisdom. You will miss a lot of opportunities if you use your brain only as a stand-alone computer. Besides, the connection is already provided, free to all, anywhere, anytime. All you need to do is practice how to use the connection.

Intuition is different from instinct. Instinct is based on our ancient learning. For example, mating has been a high priority to conserve our species, so we instinctively know "yes" and "no" signs from the opposite sex. We learned them at some point, and somehow this basic skill to distinguish the signals has been carried down through the generations. The "yes" or "no" signals, such as the way a person's eyes move, are there, however subtle they may be, and we interpret them with our instinct instantly rather than using the time-consuming process of logic.

Intuition, by contrast, is not based on observable information. It dips into the resource of information that hasn't been widely acknowledged. Sometimes, intuition tells us about things that haven't happened yet. Sometimes, intuition tells us about the people we meet for the first time and about whom we have no previous knowledge. Intuition also offers the best advice about life. Because intuition is not based on observable information, none of it can be proven. At best, it can be observed only as case studies in retrospect.

As we have seen in Chapter I, we ourselves are the one designer of this giant life simulation. So, ultimately, intuition comes from within. However, you might like to think of a third party as the source of intuition. This can help distinguish the two kinds of voices within; one is your personal voice and the other your intuition. Spirit guides and angels exist just as much as individual humans exist in this world of phenomena, so it is perfectly fine to think this way.

Developing intuition

Intuition itself is a given, but the skill to tune into intuition may need to be developed. It's like tuning into a radio signal. The signal is there and available, but you may need to practice how to tune in. Just like any learning, it's about understanding the basic ideas, dropping misunderstandings, and practice. The following is a simple approach that seems to work well, but please remember that any approach is valid as long as you get to use the connection effectively.

Although you can receive intuition anytime and anywhere, it may be helpful to have a certain setup that promotes your relaxation and awareness for the sake of practicing intuition. You want to relax because it's hard to feel anything when you are tense. But at the same time, you don't want to fall asleep. You want to have a gentle focus and alertness to notice the messages.

For many people, a private and quiet environment helps. Perhaps you want to designate a certain corner of your room as the special place to practice your intuition. If you like, you can light up a candle or incense or decorate that area with pictures or ornaments of your choice. You can also put on music as long as it's not too loud and distracting. All these elements work to condition your subconscious. The connection to the universal wisdom is provided at all times, but having a certain setup and rituals signals your subconscious that you are taking the time to connect.

Meditation also works as preparation. For this purpose, a short meditation of a few minutes is fine. You might want to visualize a special place, such as a private beach or an opening in the forest, where you feel relaxed and secure. If you like the idea of intuition coming from your angels or fairy mother, think of this place as the secret place where only you two can enter. Further, breathing is critical in relaxation. Intentionally take several deep breaths, feeling the release of tension in your body.

The potential problem with this serenity approach is that you may be one of those people who get restless in a quiet setting. So, if this approach doesn't seem to work, try something else. If the weather is nice, why not practice intuition in the garden or in the park? Or how about connecting while you take a walk (perhaps in a park so that you don't have to worry about the traffic) or while you cycle or go sailing? Being in motion, especially gentle, repetitive motion, works for quite many people.

The six pathways

Many people have fixed expectations about what intuition should be like. Are you expecting white lights hovering around you and whispering you the answer, word by word? Or a big thunderbolt showing you the direction you should take?

Intuition typically comes in a nonthreatening manner. It doesn't come as imperatives—it comes as a gentle piece of advice or reminder that you can take or leave with your free will. The exception is when you (or your loved ones) are getting into danger. Then your intuition might feel quite strong, but still not in a showy or forceful manner.

We have five physical sensory systems. With intuition, we have the equivalents of each of these plus a way to know directly without sensory information. These six pathways (or channels) of receiving spiritual messages are:

- **Clairvoyance (clear seeing):** You receive information as visual images. In other words, you see through the energetic eye what the physical eyes cannot. The image may be quite clear or blurred, color or black-and-white, still or animated. In my humble opinion, clairvoyance is overrated. It makes a great show-off but is not necessarily the most reliable method to receive intuition because seeing can be misleading.

- **Clairaudience (clear hearing):** You receive information as auditory stimulation, like a voice or music. You receive the messages through the energetic ear. Some clairaudient people hear them as if another person is talking. Others hear them as if they are recalling music or a conversation.

- **Clairsentience (clear feeling):** You receive information as physical sensations such as heat, pain, and touch. You may call this a gut feeling although the stomach is not the only area that can receive clairsentient messages.

- **Clairescence (clear smelling):** You receive information as smell. For example, your spirit guides may send you the smell of roses as a sign to start communication. For others, the same scent of roses may indicate the upcoming of a romantic encounter.
- **Clairgustance (clear tasting):** You receive information as taste.
- **Claircognizance (clear knowing):** You receive the information as direct knowing. It is like downloading a zipped file. You cannot prove it, you may not have the sensory information to supplement the case, but you just know. This is the fastest and possibly the most wholesome way to receive messages, but at the same time, it's the easiest to underestimate and ignore.

Each person has their own tendency of utilizing these pathways. You probably tend to use one or two of these channels more often than the rest. For example, your clairsentient and claircognizant senses may be more developed than your other clair senses. It's a good idea to train what you naturally tend to use rather than trying to develop your weaker senses. So in this example, I'd encourage you to train your clairsentience and claircognizance further.

Asking clear, direct, and answerable questions

A critical skill in developing intuition is forming clear, direct, and answerable questions. We are always receiving intuitive messages, but the process is quite unconscious for many of us. You might not be aware that you asked questions in your mind and that you are receiving messages in response. In order to develop the skill to consciously tune into intuition, however, we need to ask questions with intention.

The specificity of an answer can only be as good as that of the question. If you ask a vague question like "What am I supposed to do?" please do not be surprised to receive a vague, hard-to-detect answer that basically means "Whatever," or the kind of answer that you didn't expect such as "Make dinner." The universe or your spirit guides are always supportive, so when they say, "Whatever," they actually mean it in a very encouraging way. There is nothing you are supposed to do; you decide what you'd like to do. When they suggest you make dinner or take a nap, they are not ridiculing you. It's important to take good care of yourself with nutritious meals and sufficient rest, and if you don't have anything in particular to do, why not do that first?

If you would like to know, for example, whether it is beneficial for you to take the new job offer, then clearly ask so. Instead of saying, "Gosh, I am so confused. What am I supposed to do?" ask something like, "Is taking this offer in alignment with my career goal of eventually starting my own IT business?" or "Does taking this job improve my finances?" (Note the two questions can produce different responses.) Do your work of clarifying your expectations and concerns. Do not think in the line of "should"; focus on what you choose to do with your free will.

Also, notice the yes / no questions are more specific than open-ended questions. With practice, you will learn how to form clear open-ended questions, but in the beginning, yes / no questions are very helpful. Further, do not ask rhetorical questions because there is no way to answer them.

We are very used to asking half-minded, indirect questions and expecting others to figure out what we mean. When you consciously practice forming clear and direct questions, you will be surprised how challenging it is. This is a good challenge. It's about taking responsibility for your questions and your part in the conversation. Therefore, this goes far beyond intuition development. It will deepen your understanding of yourself and life in general. It will improve your relationships. The wisdom is not just in answers; it starts in questions.

How an intuitive yes and no might feel

Yes and no questions are a good place to start practicing intuition because there are only three possible answers: (1) Yes, (2) No, and (3) It doesn't matter. And when you inquire about things that you care about, you probably don't receive the third type of answer too often. So ask specific yes / no questions and pay attention to how the response feels for you.

An intuitive yes or no feels different with each person, so you can figure out how it works for you only by actually practicing this. Be lighthearted and curious like a little child who just asked a question, and start paying attention right away.

Typically, intuition comes fast. You may receive the response before you even finish your sentence.

For example, a clairvoyant might see green in their energetic eye as the indication of yes. Another clairvoyant might see the thing they asked already happening. A clairaudient might hear a certain chord or a phrase of a song that, for that person, signals yes. A clairsentient might feel the yes as a warm, expansive sensation in the chest. Another clairsentient might feel the yes as ticklishness in their right arm. A clairescence might notice a pleasant smell as yes. Likewise, a clairgustance might sense a fresh, sweet taste as the indication of yes. And a claircognizant would just know it's yes. When pressed, they might say they felt excited or liberated.

The answer no often feels like the opposite of yes, but again, everyone is different. For example, some people feel either yes or no clearly, but the other may seem vague or practically nonexistent.

These are just some examples, and your way of sensing yes and no may be quite different. The point here is to pay attention after you ask your questions and eventually recognize your signature way of feeling yes and no.

Asking "How" rather than "Why"

When you feel ready, start asking open-ended questions. When you do, refrain from asking questions that start with "why." Why questions are very close to rhetorical questions. For example, when you ask, "Why did I get into the accident?" the real sentiment behind the question is, "Why me? Why did it have to happen ever? I don't like this." You may or may not find the factual reason. For example, maybe the other driver was tired and just wasn't paying enough attention. But the point is, does this answer satisfy you? Probably not. You would then ask, "But why? Why wasn't he paying attention?" These kinds of "why" questions lead only to more "why" questions.

A more productive approach is to ask how. "How can I adjust my lifestyle so that I can still enjoy my life with this disability?" "How" questions bring your focus to what you can do now and going forward. And that is how we operate in this life simulation. Intuition is a tool to navigate forward, not a tool to dig around the path that is behind us.

The intuitive answer to your open-ended question might be some images for clairvoyants and a song or quote for clairaudients. They may be direct or symbolic. For clairsentients, clairscents, and clairgustants, the responses are typically symbolic sensations, smells, and tastes respectively, and you might need the support of claircognizant knowing to interpret them. Do not worry at this point whether it is truly intuition or just your imagination—you will find that out when you act on your intuition and receive feedback.

Practice, practice

The examples of questions I have used so far are rather serious, but when you practice intuition, start with relatively casual yet sincere questions. Nothing is too petty to ask. For example, if you have a schedule conflict, check with your intuition. When you are stuck in traffic, check intuitively if taking the backroad would get you home faster. Cannot find something? Stop searching for a moment and check with your intuition. Ask many questions, and remember to make them clear, direct, and answerable.

Also, ask the same question only once. Do not ask the same question multiple times just because you didn't like the first answer. When you do this, you are teaching your subconscious to distrust your intuition and therefore undermining your ability to tune into intuition. So form a clear and answerable question, ask, and take note. The only time when you can ask the same question again is when the situation changes significantly, and therefore, there is a good reason to assume the answer may have changed as well.

Another don't is to ask obvious questions to test your intuition. For example, do not ask, "Do I have a brother?" You already know the answer, so there is no point in using intuition about this—unless you suspect you may have a brother you are not aware of. By the same token, do not ask questions such as "What is two and three?" and "Who is the president of the United States?" Practice questions can be about petty, daily issues, but they still need to be sincere questions.

Start practicing intuition now. Using intuition only when you have to make a big decision in life is like running only when there is a big race. A smarter approach is to run often, even for short distances. This way, you get used to the process and learn the various signs your body provides. So use your intuition often. Make it part of your daily life.

Trusting intuition

Developing intuition and accessing the big wisdom is pointless unless you actually use it in your life. Your intuition development will be hindered if you don't utilize it in your real life. At first, it may be scary to trust your intuition. After all, there is no proof your intuition is accurate. You might fail. You may make a fool of yourself—although you might just as well fail not trusting intuition.

The only way to build your confidence in intuition is by using it. Action brings feedback. If it's favorable feedback, it contributes to your confidence. If it's unfavorable, you get a learning opportunity. When you take action based on intuition and things don't go as you'd hoped, there are several possible reasons:

- You confused your ego's response with intuition.
- You actually got an intuitive message accurately but waited too long to take action or modified your action.
- You got the message accurately and acted accordingly. Everything is fine. It just may not look the way you like—yet.

Sometimes we confuse our own fear as an intuitive "No." Here is the difference: an intuitive "No" is clear and definitive. It's "No." If it sounds like "Oh, no, no, no, you shouldn't do that because if you do that and fail, people will laugh at you, and you ... and ... and ...," it is your ego's fear and obsession. Intuition does not nag. Similarly, an intuitive "Yes" is clear and to the point. If it sounds like "Oh, yeah, by all means, go for it. I want it. I want it really bad. It is my right to want it. Yes, yes, yes ...," it is your ego's greed and craving.

Intuition is not euphemistic, either. While your skill to tune into intuition is underdeveloped, it may feel subtle, but intuition is never indirect, expecting you to guess what it may really mean. It may be symbolic, but the symbols you receive are the ones that are clear for you. Intuition sometimes comes in a symbolic way because symbols can contain more meanings than literal language.

Intuition doesn't justify itself or manipulate anyone. If it sounds like a lengthy sales talk, it's not intuition. And herein lies a challenge for many of us. We are so used to being persuaded with various evidence and explanations. Intuition, however, just comes and leaves without coercion. It's up to you to take it or leave it.

For example, let's say you want to improve your finances. You hold the question "How can I improve my finances?" and suddenly, you think, "Stacy" or her face may pop up in your mind. "Stacy from high school. Call her." At this point, you might think, "Huh? What does Stacy have to do with my money? I haven't even talked with her for several years ..." You probably don't get any explanation for such questions. All you get is the brief suggestion to call Stacy.

As long as it's nothing dangerous to put into practice, I recommend following your intuition. After all, what would you lose by calling Stacy? Be light-footed when it comes to intuition. If it helps, think you are just practicing intuition. In effect, a practice run is real running and practicing intuition is really using intuition, but it may help you to relax and be lighthearted.

When you act on your intuition, do not modify it. If your intuition suggests you call Stacy, call her—don't email her. And do it soon. Call her today, not this weekend. Even when you receive intuition accurately, if you don't act accordingly, you will not know how it works, and therefore, you won't be able to build your confidence in it.

At the same time, please know you don't have to follow your intuitive message. We are not robots who carry out the intuitive messages. We are humans with free will who are having the adventure of life, utilizing intuition. No one, whether you call them angels or spirit guides or God, is offended when you don't take action on your intuition. Your free will is what makes this life simulation work.

Many people want to know the difference between imagination and intuition. The two feel similar because they come through the same pathways. One of the differences is that intuition may involve knowledge that you do not have personally. In other words, intuition might sound wiser than your imaginative conversation with yourself. However, intuition can also sound very simplistic, sometimes to the point that it's childish. So the only real way to know the difference is through your own experiences of action and feedback.

When you review what happened when you acted on your intuition, try not to be too shortsighted and judgmental. Often, things are working just fine but taking longer than you'd like.

Accepting what is

It's critical that we keep our mind open to all intuitive messages. Often, we want to hear only certain answers and close up to other messages. If we keep writing off some of the messages we receive, however, we eventually get used to ignoring messages, and we begin to think we don't receive intuition.

In order to be open to all intuitive messages, we need to accept everything as it is. Acceptance doesn't mean we suck it up and sit in the corner miserably. It means we see things as they are and acknowledge them, which puts us to the real starting point. A starting point based on wishful thinking leads only to more wishful thinking, not results. Accepting things as they are is the beginning of real changes.

Acceptance may take practice. It seems to be ingrained in many of us to resist what is, and changing this mind habit might take some training of its own. If this is the case with you, please work on it before utilizing intuition. In other words, do not ask questions if you are not ready to hear answers you may not like. For example, if you ask, "Are there ways to restore me to full health, or will I have this health problem for the rest of my life?" you will receive an intuitive response, and the response may be that, indeed, you will be sick for a very long time. Or the message may be that you need to radically change your lifestyle to get better, which you might not like, either.

Denial does not change what is. It only takes you to a fantasy land that exists only in your mind. Living in that fantasy land while ignoring reality is a form of insanity. It drains your life energy, the energy that flows from the Source for your life in this reality. When we accept what is with love and courage, we establish our step in wisdom.

How to read your own Akashic Records

Psychic reading is nothing more than well-developed intuition. This book is not intended to be about psychic development, but for those who are interested, here is an introduction to reading your own Akashic Records. Please use it to deepen your understanding of yourself.

Reading your own Akashic Records doesn't require you to access the Hall of the Akashic Records, where all the Akashic Records are stored. You carry the energetic copy of your own Akashic Records. So, reading your own Akashic Records is not particularly difficult, but still there are some prerequisites. One is the ability to get into a meditative state. While the regular intuition can come in a casual way, reading the Akashic Records takes a little more focus. You need to be able to set aside your current thoughts and be open to whatever information you may find.

The other prerequisite is the willingness to reveal and accept whatever is recorded about yourself. You might receive disturbing information, such as the way you died in one of your past lives or some serious problems that bothered you for a long time back then—and how you yourself contributed to the problem. If, in your daily life, you tend to avoid problems or neglect challenges, how can you face such information when you read your Akashic Records?

Although it is not a prerequisite, compassionate understanding of humanity and its history is also helpful to make the reading meaningful. For example, let's say you find you were a slave driver in your past life. If you think this is horrible and close your heart, the reading ends there. Being a slave driver, however, doesn't automatically mean you were a mean and cruel person. Maybe you tried to treat them as kindly and fairly as possible, but because you were only the middle management and not the owner, there wasn't much you could do. And perhaps this dilemma is the reason why you feel hesitant to accept the promotion to management position now—you are afraid of getting into the same kind of dilemma. A reading can only be as deep as your understanding of life.

To start the reading session of your Akashic Records, you might want to have a certain ritual. Doing some preparatory meditation is a good idea. Voicing your intention is also a good practice. Say something like, "Let the energy of Love, Light, and Truth prevail on Earth. My spirit guides, please help me open my Akashic Records so that I may have the wisdom to live this life with more awareness and courage." The "Love, Light, and Truth" part is essential. You are making it clear that you are doing this reading with love, not judgments; with light (spiritual awareness), not confusion; and for truth, rather than hiding in untruth or ignorance. In other words, you are saying that you are open to the truth, whatever it may be, and you are willing to receive it with love and light.

I do not recommend reading the Akashic Records with sheer curiosity because it won't be very productive. If you just ask, "What was I doing in my past life?" you could receive information regarding any of your many past lives, regardless of how influential that lifetime may be to your present life. The answer would probably be uninteresting and vague. Like any intuitive inquiries, the inquiry for the Akashic Records needs to be clear and direct. So please read the Akashic Records for problem solving. For example, you might want to ask something like, "This (brief description of your issue) is what I've been working on, and I feel there is something more than I know in my present life. If this is true, please provide the information of when and how this problem originated."

Just like any intuitive messages, the way you receive the information depends on which of your clairs is most developed. You might see a picture or video clip in your energetic eye. You might hear music that symbolizes something. You might feel it, smell it, or taste it. You might just know. Or perhaps it will be the combination of a few of these. Receive the information, ask some additional clarifying questions if you need to, and then close the session with gratitude. You receive just as much information as is helpful for you now.

How will you know if you have received accurate information? It will resonate and make sense to you. You might even experience changes. Although this doesn't happen with every accurate reading, I have heard interesting cases, such as pains dissipating or relationships improving or ending for no apparent reason. There are also people who temporarily feel down, such as by catching a cold, before they feel better.

There are, however, special cases when the accurate reading does not resonate at all—in fact, you'd be tempted to deny the reading by all means. It's when the reading reveals the most uncomfortable truth about yourself. If this happens, it's a good idea not to go back to denial. Getting this uncomfortable reading can be the start of changing your life—if you so choose.

A few additional cautions: Especially in the beginning, keep your reading session brief. The Akashic Records contain an astronomical amount of information, so it's critical to keep your focus. Otherwise, you could get overwhelmed by the various pieces of information. This can result in inaccuracy in reading, and further, your brain can get overloaded. Do not get carried away with curiosity.

While we are discussing the Akashic Records, allow me to caution you not to read other people's Akashic Records unless you have their explicit consent. We share the information and insights in the Akashic Records, but this doesn't mean you are entitled to compromise others' privacy. Reading the Akashic Records is like walking into someone's house and looking around. If it's your own house, you obviously have the right to do this. You own even the things you have forgotten to be there, so you have the right to open the boxes and check their contents. With other people's houses, however, you don't just walk in and snoop around. Even when your intention is benevolent, it is not yours to do so. A minor exception is those who are significant in your life, like your family members. With them, you may read their Akashic Records to the extent that is relevant to you.

Those who force their way in to gain information in the Akashic Records may receive inaccurate information, information that sounds right and is probably close to truth but not entirely true. This is why some books on the Akashic Records or the past life regression sound unnecessarily complicated. They are weaving reliable and inaccurate information together.

The Akashic Records are our shared resource throughout the history of this universe. Perhaps, when this universe ends and another one starts with another Big Bang, we will have another set of the Akashic Records. Until then, please treat this energetic record with respect.

The wisdom of not needing to know

Intuition is wonderful as it provides knowledge and wisdom beyond what we can learn through ordinary approaches. Yet, what is even more important than developing intuition is cultivating the sense of adventure and discovery in life. If you knew all the answers, there would not be much point in being alive and playing this giant life simulation game. There is wisdom in being okay with not knowing why something is happening or what may be waiting on the way. Knowing what to find out, by intuition or other approaches, and what to leave unknown is the true essence of wisdom.

If you tend to ask more and more questions as you receive answers, you might want to stop and check your intention. Do you intend to use the wisdom in your real life, or are you asking questions for the sake of asking questions while you postpone the application of the wisdom in your life? In other words, is your motivation courage or fear? As we reviewed, intuition does not explain why you might want to do something. When you keep asking probing questions out of fear, the answers tend to come from the ego, not intuitive connection. So you get more and more confused.

Please also understand that intuitive wisdom comes on an as-needed basis. For instance, you cannot have all the intuitive messages for a project from beginning to end up front before you even start that project. That would totally defy the nature of this life simulation, which is about adventure and exploration.

Often, the wisest thing to do in the big picture appears to be counterproductive to your short-term benefits. This is why it is best to realize our loving nature first. The Source energy's primary nature is love. When we realize we are love, we can utilize intuitive wisdom even when it appears to be counterproductive for oneself. Love helps us understand the big wisdom that the ego has no way to comprehend. Moving forward, love and wisdom need to be exercised in this reality, which takes strength and power.

COURAGE TO BE POWERFUL

*All the powers in the universe
are already ours.
It is we who have put our hands
before our eyes and cry that it is dark.*
— Swami Vivekananda

Owning our inner power

We are afraid of many things in life. Getting into a relationship is scary. Leaving a relationship is scary. Losing a job is scary. Starting a business is scary. Not having enough money is scary. Just having money and being found to be an empty person is scary. Traveling alone is scary. Speaking in public is scary. And so on. But remember, we all have done the scariest thing already: being born in this world of phenomena. That took an incredible amount of courage and power.

As spirit, we are already One and we know love. We know everything and all the wisdom. This ideal condition, however, wasn't enough for us. So we have chosen to experience love rather than just knowing it. For this grand purpose, we have set up this reality, a stage where we can exercise our power to apply our wisdom so that we can experience love. Empowerment is an aspect of the Source energy. Because we are connected to the Source, this power is already within us. All we need to do is realize it and start utilizing it. We need to allow ourselves to be fully powerful.

When we don't embrace this innate power, our love eventually withers. It becomes a nice idea, not something we can actually experience in this world of phenomena. We will also lose our wisdom when we don't own our power. Certain situations ask us to take action with our inner power, and the only way we can avoid exercising our power is either to close our eyes to the situation or justify the situation with some twisted logic. If we close our eyes to one situation, we eventually close our eyes to other situations, and we become mentally blind, losing the light of wisdom. If we use twisted logic for one situation, we eventually apply that to other situations, twisting our mind and wisdom. By embracing the power of the Source, we can see through even the disturbing situations and keep our mind open and balanced. Thus, the power supports the other two aspects of the Source energy, love and wisdom.

While we can never lose our innate power, we can forget about it and believe we are powerless. When you believe you are powerless, you quit exercising your power, and your belief of your powerlessness is reinforced. We even start fearing power and the responsibility that any power brings, believing they are some monstrous, unmanageable things. Further, when you quit utilizing your own power, someone else has to do it for you, and consequently, you start relying on others' power. A soul with full innate power pretending to be powerless and depending on others is unhealthy to say the least, ridiculous perhaps, and sooner or later will cause resentment on both sides.

No one has taken away your power. That is impossible. If you feel someone is pushing you around with their power, the situation is serving you as the wake-up call to remember your own power.

External powers

When we are unaware of our innate power, we seek power outside ourselves. However, such a search is destined to fail:

either we fail to acquire the power that we believe to exist outside ourselves, or we successfully acquire such seeming power only to realize it is not real power.

Authority is a good example of such fake power that seems to exist outside ourselves. Most people who seek to have authority believe in the power of authority themselves. In other words, they believe there are right ways and wrong ways to do things, or the way people should follow and the way people shouldn't. So they seek established authorities themselves. They try hard to learn the ins and outs of the authority and relinquish their own authentic thinking. Eventually, they make their way in the shiny line of authorities, and by then, they forget their own authentic power. So they become more like puppets of authoritative power. Most people in authority—those who are bowed to and feared by many people—are secretly afraid because they know their power is dependent on following a certain code. They know the hollow nature of the authoritative power, which drives some of them to be more manipulative.

In a sense, those who are not in the position of authority are better positioned to embrace their own innate power. When an authoritative person thinks for themselves and makes a decision that doesn't agree with the established "should," their decision is usually called a mistake and criticized openly and harshly. Of course, this is still possible, and it is the only way for them to break away from the fake power of authority to get back to the true power of the Source. (Please note that there are some who have acquired authority not because they have bought into it themselves but because they embraced their own uniqueness. There are only a handful of such exceptional cases, but the few that do exist are notable.)

True empowerment brings freedom, or empowerment and freedom are two sides of the same condition. You cannot be truly free while you are dependent on external power; freedom requires that you take up your own power. Only when you accept your power and its responsibilities will you be free, and your sense of freedom deepens your awareness of inner power. Be open to seeing this world with your own untainted eyes, free from conventional ideas. Think for yourself and trust your intuition. And be thrilled to step forward—this life is an adventure in the giant simulation.

Problems are opportunities

Do you wish you had no problems? When we understand why we have taken the trouble to incarnate in this so-called reality, however, problems have new meanings: opportunities. Your problems are a critical part of your life plan, which you yourself created prior to birth. Once you achieve a certain success and enjoy it for a while, you are best off moving on to another creative project. Just in case we forget to do this voluntarily, we have incorporated some reminders in our life plan, which appear to be problems.

We are supposed to have problems. This doesn't mean life has to be a continual series of suffering; suffering is the ego's reaction to problems. For the soul, problems are challenges, like challenges in a good game. As the brave souls we really are, we receive problems, and eventually, we come to enjoy them.

Therefore, problems are not really caused by others. We ourselves set them up and then forget about them. The people who appear to have caused you problems are only playing their roles, as you yourself play your role, according to various agreements. These agreements are flexible and allow many options, which is where our free will comes into play. For example, if you voluntarily move on to a new project, then there is no need for someone to cause a problem for you so that you will have to move on.

Rejection is one such reminder that we usually consider a problem. It is in our best interest to consider rejection as a kind of road sign that redirects us to another route, a route that eventually leads to a new experience of love and joy. It doesn't work for us to just coast along the same route. We either initiate turns ourselves, or rejections and other problems redirect us.

Appreciating problems may be a foreign idea to many people. Our ego, which is about survival, hates problems and doesn't understand the meaning of them. However, for the soul, problems are opportunities to exercise its power, wisdom, and love. We don't need to be afraid of problems because we receive only as many problems as we can handle on an ongoing basis. Again, it is we ourselves who have planned them. Once we fully understand how each problem is an opportunity in our life, they cease to be problems. We don't really solve problems; we disintegrate problems by turning them inside out and using them as opportunities.

Nurturing creativity

How can we start appreciating problems as opportunities? Ultimately, this is about disidentifying with the ego, but we can start the process in a fun way: by nurturing our creativity.

You are creative even if you are not an artist—because the power that is flowing in you from the Source is creative. It's the power that created the universe and everything in it, including us. We, in turn, use this creative power to create our own lives. We first set up all the possibilities for our life and then, once incarnated, choose one possible option after another with our free will, creating new combinations. We are always doing this, but problems urge us to do this creative process consciously.

And so, it is a good idea to exercise our creativity daily before major problems present themselves. We can learn a great deal from small children here. Have you seen a small kid who is not creative? They are always playing, aren't they? They love to doodle and color. They love to sing and dance, to make up their lyrics and music. They love to play make-believe games—they can be anything instantly in their mind. Everyday objects become toys, and routines become fun activities. They cannot even finish dinner without playing with their food.

The life simulation is not much different from children's make-believe games, so the skill is transferable. We want to relax and be attentive at the same time. Curiosity helps, too, because creativity is essentially about trying new combinations with the spirit of "Okay, what happens if I do this?" We don't really know, but we can make a guess and then see if our guess works.

Creativity converts problems into opportunities for expression. A challenge presents itself, we experiment doing what we can at this time, and we see what happens. Next time when a similar challenge happens, we might try another approach, but for now, we improvise in this here and now.

As we practice creativity, we become more and more aware of who we are. We find that each person works on the problem in their unique, authentic way. It doesn't mean one approach is better than others. One song can be played in various ways, and we can enjoy others' improvisations while we also enjoy our own. By promoting authenticity, creative fun guides us on our own unique life path.

Little creative fun leads to the big creative power to change your life and the world because it is essentially the same creative energy. So take time for creative fun, especially when you are busy and overwhelmed.

Power and sensitivity

Problems are an essential part of our life, but this doesn't mean we shouldn't be helping others because "they chose such problems themselves." First, there is nothing we should or shouldn't do; instead, everything is about how we choose to handle it. We are here to experience love and its various aspects, and helping others may well be the path to do this. In a sense, they may be presenting themselves with supersized problems so that people around them can experience compassion.

We are very desensitized these days. Some people even watch murder for entertainment—on the screen. Such people may ridicule sensitive souls as naive, as if being insensitive is the sign of wisdom and strength. Don't give in to such peer pressure. Robots have no sensitivity, but that is not what we aspire to be. True power of life embraces sensitivity and compassion. True power is not arrogant.

True power is also patient and tolerant. We know this from experience. Patience takes a sustained output of power—it's much easier to throw a tantrum. Tolerance takes resilience in power, or depth in power, and again, jumping to short-circuited judgment is easier. Impatience and intolerance even resort to violence occasionally, which might appear to be powerful, but in truth, most use of violence is rooted in cowardice.

Fake powers have undesirable attributes such as insensitivity, arrogance, impatience, and intolerance. If you have associated such qualities with power, please take time to contemplate what true power might mean and release the misunderstanding with love and wisdom. You cannot embrace your own power wholeheartedly while you also think power is dirty.

Feeling the full spectrum of emotions

In order to fully embrace our inner power, we first need to accept all emotions rather than ignoring certain emotions that we think are too weak, bad, or negative. Suppressing emotions doesn't end them; it just buries the emotions under the surface. So the suppressed emotions are waiting for their chance to come back. This is why some people feel the same fear, anger, and sorrow repeatedly—and sometimes quite unexpectedly.

In other words, when you judge and suppress emotions, you become your own threatening enemy from whom you can never get away. You also miss feeling joy and happiness because all emotions come through the same pathway. Suppressing one emotion means suppressing all emotions. Consequently, your life shrinks as your feelings shrink. In contrast, if you dare to feel all emotions, you will soon find that the emotions pass quite quickly.

So be open and vulnerable and feel everything without judgments. Then, practice appropriate expression of the emotions. For example, feeling anger by itself is healthy, but expressing the anger with violence is not. We don't need anger management skills; we need appropriate anger expression skills. This may include taking time off, reflecting on your own or with compassionate third parties, expressing through sports performance or arts, to name a few.

All emotions are just signals. Take note, understand what each signal means, and take appropriate actions and expressions, and they will pass.

Fear and anger

Emotions are signals. Joy signals that you are doing something that resonates with the natural flow of life and therefore encourages you to do more of it. Anger, on the other hand, warns us that our boundary is compromised and therefore encourages us to take action for our safety. It is like a smoke alarm. Although the alarm may sound noisy and annoying, we don't want to deactivate it or ignore it. Doing so would be counterproductive to our life. Once we take note of the alarm and take appropriate action, it stops. This may include recalibrating oversensitive alarms.

Fear also signals that something may be threatening our well-being. It is natural to feel fear when the brake of your car doesn't seem to be working, for example. Because change can be risky, any change can activate fear, even though some changes are actually good for us. Growth is a type of change, so young people are often scared, and you can stay young by mentally growing, which might involve a level of continued fear. It is quite typical to feel fear when we start a new project. The fear doesn't mean the project is a bad idea—it may be the perfect project to experience your purpose.

Further, we feel extreme fear when we are about to disidentify with the ego. The ego is indeed threatened to lose its control over our life. This is a wonderful fear—we are finally remembering who we really are. Move through this fear. When you completely disidentify with the ego, this type of fear is replaced with a greater sense of love and peace of the soul, based on the understanding that we don't need to control our life. Then you will no longer be afraid of being afraid. This is when you finally realize that all fear was coming from the ego.

The ego thinks others are against it. When the ego thinks it is weaker than its perceived opponent, it feels fear. When the ego thinks it might be as strong as its opponent, it feels anger and starts a fight. The ego doesn't understand that true power comes from the Source, which embraces us all. The ego also thinks events and situations can be against it, so it makes hasty and superficial judgments and gets afraid or upset. The ego does not understand all things happen for us.

Once you disidentify with the ego, the fear of the new is replaced with excitement, joy, and even the sense of magic. The fear of being judged by others becomes irrelevant because you feel your unconditional love for them. Even the fear caused by physical danger changes. Your body might still get triggered and respond with symptoms such as tension, but when you truly realize you are a soul, which doesn't die at physical death, you are not afraid in the same way.

It is essential to understand that you first need to feel the fear of disidentifying with the ego in order to disidentify with the fear of the ego. This process may also involve anger because the ego's boundary is indeed violated. This is not about choosing love over fear and anger. Choosing love is a good principle in our social life, but when it comes to how you really feel, you need to feel everything without labeling. Pretending you have disidentified with the ego prevents real disidentification with the ego, as we reviewed in Chapter II.

Grief and its variations

Grief is another emotion that is often disliked and suppressed. Grief is not just about feeling sad. It is a signal that something or someone that is significant to us is lost. It may be the death of a loved one, the end of a relationship or career, or even the loss of a treasured item. When the loss is about the intangible or about things with low monetary value, some people try to ignore their grief, but this is a shallow understanding. Grief is the emotional signal that we need to take time to adjust to the new life without what is lost. Do take sufficient time for grief. Cry. Share your memories of what is lost. Just like taking a rest after physical injury promotes recovery, taking time to grieve promotes recovery.

We even grieve over the loss of anticipated events, that is, something we never had but hoped to have. It's called disappointment. In other words, regular grief is grief over the past and disappointment is grief over the future. As we allow ourselves to feel these emotions, we eventually realize we are living now—without the beloved people or things, or the cherished dream—and still, we are here and alive ourselves. At this point, we can feel the power of life.

Another variation of grief is sympathy, feeling for someone who is going through grief. Sympathy is very human. Our highly developed ability to sense and imagine others' pain makes sympathy possible. The same ability also makes it possible for us to share joy, to celebrate someone's success as if it were our own. It is one of the many ways we realize our Oneness.

In the greater reality, nothing is lost; the energy only changes forms, from manifest to unmanifest to another manifest. The totality of the Source energy stays the same. When we really understand this—not just intellectually but intuitively—grief changes to something like a transparent farewell. We held each other's hands for a while in this giant dance of life, then we let go of each other and met another, and this dance keeps going on beyond physical deaths and births. We know we will meet again, perhaps in a different kind of relationship, as we have been doing so many times already.

What feeling down really means

Feeling sad or down is the result of suppressing other emotions. For many people, sadness is more acceptable than anger or fear. So instead of getting upset at someone who annoys you, for example, you might feel sad about the situation. Instead of feeling scared and anxious about speaking up in public, for example, you might feel blue about the prospect of having to make the presentation. This is why those who attempt to appear holier than others by suppressing their emotions are actually very sad and depressed.

This swap process of emotions is often paired with blaming. Blaming is about pushing the responsibility around. If you properly feel anger, you get up and take action with your own power. This means you accept the responsibility of your action. In contrast, when you suppress your anger and twist it, you blame someone. You pretend the responsibility is theirs. Of course, this doesn't improve anything, so you feel disempowered and sad. Likewise, when you acknowledge and own your fear, you recognize your current limitation and you take responsibility for that. But some people swap the fear and blame someone else. This way they don't feel the fear; instead, they feel frustrated and disempowered.

When you repeat this swapping enough times and it becomes automatic and unconscious, you will find you are sad and bitter most of the time and unhappiness becomes your regular habitat. Occasionally, some luck might take you up to happiness, but because it wasn't you who made yourself happy, you stay feeling powerless, and you fall down to your repressed state of unhappiness soon.

Some people suppress their feelings even further and blame themselves rather than others. This way, they can play the blaming game all on their own. Blaming oneself, however, is fundamentally different from taking an honest look at the situation and owning your responsibility. Like all blaming, it is based on twisted logic and therefore counterproductive.

Sadness, other than grief, is not really an emotion of its own but a distress of emotions. Therefore, the solution is to let yourself feel all emotions. It may be scary and overwhelming, especially in the beginning, and you might need assistance as you learn how to accept and take care of all feelings.

Emotional healing

We can even heal our old emotional wounds by allowing ourselves to feel the pain now. Unlike a glass vase, we have natural healing power within us. It brings optimal healing to both physical and emotional wounds. The trouble for many of us is that we haven't learned how to utilize this healing power for emotional wounds.

Emotional wounds cause pain just as physical wounds do. Pain is a signal that calls for our attention. When we take note of the pain and take appropriate care, including resting and removing the cause of further wounds, healing works best. However, many people are afraid of the pain and try to cover it up. Some people pop painkiller drugs for physical pain and mood-altering drugs (some legal and some illegal) for emotional pain. Such drugs don't heal. In fact, they may cause an additional problem of addiction due to their chemical effects and the fact that the underlying wounds stay untreated. Others cover up their pain with activities, such as overworking and shopping, which also don't heal and may become addictive. When you only cover up the wound and pretend to rise above the pain, you end up feeling the same old pain repeatedly—new situations, maybe with different people, but the same old fear, anger, and resentment over and over again.

Rather, why not look into the pain and accompanying emotions? At first glance, it may appear that the pain is inflicted by someone. Then you will notice the part of yourself that is really causing the pain and therefore needs healing. For example, let's say you feel hurt because someone called you stupid. Perhaps they really didn't need to make such mean comments over a simple mistake you made. You might feel upset at that person or people like them in general. And you might feel afraid of receiving similarly unkind comments. Then, when you look in further, you will notice the part of you that is bothered with that comment. If you are absolutely confident of your intelligence, you won't feel bad at being called stupid. You might be puzzled: "Someone thinks I am stupid?" This is not about putting up a tough facade and pretending you don't mind mean criticism while, in fact, you are feeling hurt. This is about the same kind of amazement you might feel when someone seriously insists that the Earth is flat. You'd have no emotional investment—you'd just wonder how they could possibly come up with that idea.

The fact that you feel one way or the other about someone's comment about you means that there is a part in you that is already wounded. If you secretly suspect you might be stupid, you will react to others' comments about it. It is not about them, but about that part of yourself. We can even thank that person for letting us know which part of ourselves needs healing.

So, in this example, really look into yourself and ask if you are indeed stupid. At first, your ego will throw in many answers. It might automatically bark back, "No, no, no." Or it might say something like, "Well, my aunt once made that same comment when I was five ... and my third grade teacher ...," or "I did make a big mistake in that group project—everyone was upset at me." Do not analyze any of the ego's responses. Do not respond; just let them pass. Keep asking yourself if you are really stupid and what stupidity means. Does making mistakes signify stupidity? Or does it mean you tried something?

Eventually, you will find yourself thinking less of what others have said to you. You will be thinking more of what you think of yourself. At this point, you have gained full healing power, and the initial mean comment will feel so irrelevant that it is laughable. Work on this emotional healing every time you feel hurt rather than ignoring the hurt feeling or reacting to the person who appears to have hurt you. You might also want to look into your Akashic Records to gain deeper clarity about why you feel the way you do.

Additionally, you might want to do the same when you feel overexcited and overjoyed when someone praises you or when things appear to be working favorably for you. Feeling overexcited with praises is only the flip side of feeling hurt with put-downs. You don't need to deny it—you can accept the praise with grace. Just know who you are whether people praise you or criticize you.

Ultimately, emotional healing is not just about feeling better. It is one of the paths to disidentifying with the ego, similar to the path of suffering, as we reviewed in Chapter II, but taken one step at a time. Eventually, you will recover to your original wholeness. You will realize you are not the ego, which reacts to various stimulations. You are the all-powerful, all-knowing, loving soul.

Healing for empaths

Some people pick up others' emotions and feelings, especially painful feelings, energetically. For example, they might sense their friend is feeling anxious even when the friend says nothing about it and pretends to be fine. They might even pick up strangers' feelings when they go into a crowd. These empaths are not necessarily compassionate for those who are going through tough times—they just pick up others' feelings in an uncontrolled manner.

Or we can say there are two types of empaths. One is those who are skilled in picking up and understanding others' feelings. They consciously open their channel to the person who is asking for assistance, pick up the client's feelings energetically, then close their channel. They can do this because they also know how to heal emotional wounds. The other is the unconscious type described above. They don't know how to open and close their channel, and they don't know what to do with the information they pick up. Consequently, they are rather unhappy about their empathic tendency.

When you ignore your true feelings and therefore unknowingly carry untreated emotional wounds, the hidden feelings and pains resonate with the same kind of feelings of others. We are all silently signaling out our thoughts and feelings, and when the signal finds a similar wavelength, it resonates and becomes bigger. Even though the aforementioned empath might think they were feeling perfectly fine until they went to the shopping mall and picked up loads of others' feelings, for instance, the energetic truth is that they themselves have been carrying the same feelings that they picked up. Thus, they are urged to heal their own emotional wounds that they have been ignoring.

There seems to be a certain excitement when someone can do things that our current science cannot explain, such as this empathic energy collection. As you may have noticed, however, the uncontrolled empathic capacity is no sign of well-developed intuition or spirituality. If you are this type of empath, the solution is to dare to look within. Staying away from a crowd may be a good idea in the meantime, but it is not the ultimate long-term solution.

Energetic protection

Much has been discussed about energetic protection or psychic shields, such as "visualizing a purple light around oneself" or "putting on a psychic armor of mirrors." But here is the innate dilemma of such protection: it assumes we can be energetically attacked without such protection. When we accept this assumption, however, we shift our focus from love to fear, thus making ourselves susceptible to such attacks, which makes us feel we need such protection.

Energetic attacks such as curses and spells cannot affect us until we ourselves buy into them. Anyone can send out malicious energies just as they can send out the warm, expansive energy of love. They can even direct the energy to a specific person or persons. This is up to each soul's free will. However, if you don't pick up the harmful energy, it cannot do any harm to you. There are basically two cases why people pick up undesirable energies. One is when you are the kind of empath who doesn't know how to consciously open and close your channel. The other is when you secretly feel bad about what you have done and therefore energetically accept the blame for it. In both cases, what is really necessary is your healing, not energetic defense.

In other words, love is the best protection. When we love ourselves completely, including all our emotions and deeds, the love heals us, which makes it impossible for others to energetically harm us. While you are at it, send love to those who are sending out the energetic attacks. This neutralizes the harmful energy and gives the optimal opportunity of healing to those who are sending it out. After all, if they knew how to experience love and joy regardless of what happens to them, they would choose that rather than feeling miserable and sending out the poor vibes.

This principle of loving all but not participating in others' energetic dramas works in more practical cases as well. You don't need to get rid of so-called toxic people in your life. When you quit engaging in the emotional tug-of-war with them, they either drop their end of the rope or they disappear on their own. It is we who are keeping them around, trying to defend and prove ourselves, reacting to every move they make. You don't even need to judge who the toxic people are in your life. Just focus on your own love and light.

We are born with layers of light around us. This is why many religious figures are painted within a white or golden bubble, or sometimes layers of bubbles. This natural insulation is all we need; we don't need to put on an additional energetic shield. While the natural layer of light is made of love and allows love to pass in and out, an artificial shield blocks everything. You may feel better temporarily, but in the long run, you will feel isolated.

Self-esteem is unnecessary

Self-esteem is often considered necessary for empowerment, but that is the case when you try to empower the ego. Self-esteem is usually about the small self, the ego, because that is how we typically see ourselves. In order to empower the ego, the ego needs to feel it is better than others. This ego boost is delusional, however, because we are all parts of one big life. Therefore, power based on self-esteem is fragile and only lasts as long as the delusion lasts.

While the ego works against others, or works with a select group of people in order to work against others outside the group, true power works with all others. This means that, to utilize this power, we need to realize conflicts are superficial and temporary. If I am seeing conflicts, then it is me who need to humbly review my perspective and figure out a better way of working. This includes taking the answer "No" gracefully rather than forcing my way. True power works with love and wisdom. It brings win-win results because if someone is losing, we are all losing as a whole.

You may be wondering how we deal with criticisms if we have no self-esteem. We do this by listening and sincerely trying to understand the perspective of those who criticize us. Also, we will look into their eyes. If you really look into the eyes of someone who is criticizing others, you will see their own anger, frustration, and even fear. They are only expressing their anger that their boundaries would be disrespected and their way might disintegrate. It's not really about you. At this point, of course, you can have mercy on them.

Let us learn to live and let live. Nobody is better or worse than anyone else, but each of us is experimenting in this giant life simulation game in their own unique way. Let's respect others' perspectives and way of life as much as our own.

Nothing to forgive

Forgiveness is a strange idea. It assumes there is something and someone to be forgiven. In other words, we assume something went wrong. This is a judgment based on our perception. Sure, we may not like it. We might feel hurt. But then, feeling hurt can be the long-awaited opportunity to heal the old wounds we have been carrying around—if we choose to utilize this opportunity. This, of course, doesn't mean we can abuse or attack someone because "good or bad is only a judgment call." It means, if you have been on the receiving side of abuse, you have the strength to recover and to employ the experience for higher good.

In practice, we probably have to forgive before we come to this understanding. This is internal work because judgment is within. Forgiveness doesn't mean we tell the offender that we forgive them and make friends with them. It is the process of releasing the underlying judgment. It probably takes many attempts. Even when you decide to forgive someone, the next day you might find yourself feeling the same old resentment again. So you forgive again. And again.

Many of us, however, make the secondary mistake of replaying that hurtful drama in our mind repeatedly, as if we can change the past event by coming up with the counteraction later. This is a habitual mind game many of us play with ourselves. The offender may not be doing anything anymore, but we ourselves keep peeling off our healing scab. Blaming is usually part of this self-inflicted wound. Blaming is about pushing responsibilities around, and as we have seen, so long as we avoid power and responsibility, nothing gets resolved. The way out is accepting exactly what happened and who you are now, including that experience. Is victim your identity, or are you someone whose experience includes that experience? Do you choose to remain the mental victim of your thoughts, or do you choose to move on, perhaps even stronger, wiser, and more compassionate with that experience?

You may also need to forgive yourself for the things you have done. Again, this involves judgment, but we need to be completely honest with ourselves in releasing this judgment.

Just saying, "Well, I didn't really do anything wrong. Nothing is wrong. It's all judgment," does not work. If you honestly don't feel good about what you have done, it means you did something that is out of alignment with yourself, and you need to make a sincere effort not to do it again. You might also want to make amends with the people that your action has affected, if such amends are possible and welcomed.

Then you learn generosity one step at a time. Generosity is providing love and kindness to those you think undeserving. So generosity defies judgment. When you are generous and learn to forgive others, you become more forgiving to yourself. We cannot forgive ourselves while judging others. In turn, when we are generous and forgiving to ourselves, we are open to offer the same generosity and forgiveness to others.

At some point, you will realize there is nothing to forgive. This is not about denial. When you deeply and completely love yourself, you find there is nothing to forgive because everyone and everything has contributed to who you are now. Forgiveness is replaced with acceptance and love.

Expressing our divinity

Because we tend to identify with the ego, which is full of limitations and knows only the kind of power that is exercised against one another, we tend to play small in this life simulation game. Don't. You are not your ego. You are the spark of the Source, and within you lies the same divinity that created the whole universe.

Playing big in the life simulation is not about being ambitious for worldly success. Worldly success is fine if it is something that you really enjoy, but far bigger than any fame and wealth is to manifest your inner divinity. To do this, you don't have to wait until you acquire a certain social status or position, and you don't need to do some showy and heroic act.

You can start right now by being kind to those who are indifferent and helping those whom you have thought to have wronged you. Bless those whom your ego condemns undeserving and forgive those you think unforgivable. Kindness to your friends is common sense. Go beyond such limitations and challenge yourself to be kind to even one stranger, or one person you find unkind and mean. When you do, you are stepping out of the ego's limitation and acting as God would.

"Deserving" is yet another judgment call after all. The truth is we all deserve, or nobody deserves anything but everything is given on grace. For example, have I done any good to deserve a priceless gift such as my vision or even one tooth? No. Everything in my life, and my life itself, is given as a gift. And if my life is a gift, so is everyone else's life. Do not consume yourself thinking about who deserves what. Just do the best you can to be kind indiscriminately.

Eventually, you realize you are not doing it for others—you are actually healing yourself. When you are kind to those who are indifferent, you are healing the part of you that has grown cold and reserved. When you help those who have wronged you, you are releasing your own sense of guilt and your judgments.

Whatever you do to others, you automatically do to yourself because, ultimately, there is only one being.

If you think it would be too difficult to be so generous and do these things, it is all the more reason to give it a shot. Your inner power and divinity is waiting for expression. Again, don't play small and stay within the limitation of common sense reciprocity. Do more because you are more than you think you are.

Follow your challenge

"Follow your bliss" is common advice, but most people misunderstand what bliss means. If you think bliss is about easygoing and temporary good feeling, you might want to follow your challenge instead. Think for a moment: Did Jesus follow his bliss? Did Mother Teresa follow her bliss? Did Van Gogh?

As we reviewed in Chapter III, each soul chooses an aspect of love as their life theme, or their personal purpose for the upcoming lifetime. The life theme is often reflected in one's challenges. Sometimes we choose to be born into an environment that lacks the aspect of love we are working to experience, so that we first know what it is like not to have it. Sometimes we choose challenges later in life that serve as a kind of jump-board. For example, a soul that intends to experience self-trust or autonomy may get into situations that force them to doubt themselves. When they successfully go through such difficulties, they experience strong self-trust.

Because our purpose assumes some challenges, a scary plan is a great plan. The thing that you really came to do will give you some trepidation. If it's easy, there is not much point in doing it, just as there is not much point in playing tic-tac-toe anymore. The thing that you came to do will give you the kind of trepidation that comes from knowing that, even though it may take an enormous amount of effort and trials, you just might make it, and the vision of its achievement feels awesome. It borders on dream and reality. And the efforts are not drudgery—for you, they are interesting and exciting work.

So follow your challenge—not the challenge that requires you to masochistically take abuse, but the challenge that stretches you to be stronger so that you manifest your inner greatness. That's what Van Gogh did; he continued painting even after many rejections and criticisms. And in a sense, he did follow his bliss at the same time. He wanted to paint more than anything. Mother Teresa also followed her bliss. She chose to live in service, fully knowing it would bring challenges, and at the same time, the life of service was her highest delight. If bliss means this much deep joy, following your bliss and following your challenge are the same.

Following your challenge doesn't mean you force your way. That's the way of the ego. You can follow your challenge as you approach an adventure—with fresh curiosity and a sense of discovery, testing your limit because it is fun.

The story of the babies who refused to be born

Granted, showing up in life takes courage. Just being born takes courage. Our power is always within us, but we need to take the courage to embrace this power.

Let's wrap up this chapter with a short story, which I hope illustrates the point.

This story may sound like something that would happen in the future, but time is a loop, and what may happen in the future might have happened already.

People noticed there were fewer and fewer babies being born. At first, they just heard of couples having trouble to conceive. They felt sorry for such couples, but they didn't pay much attention. Then they heard of their friends, or friends of friends, having the same problem. The news started to spread that there were fewer new babies.

People seldom saw babies in restaurants and parks any longer. They realized how much joy they were receiving from seeing babies, even strangers' babies. They felt sad and worried, but they didn't know what to do.

The governments encouraged people to have babies. Various scientific studies were done to increase fertility. Yet the number of new babies kept decreasing.

Finally, the day came when no baby was born in the world.

People prayed. They found a sage who could go to the land of unborn babies and asked her to go talk to them.

Her spirit flew through the night sky and went to the land of dawn, where the spirits of babies to be born lived.

"Hello, dear babies," the sage said. "It seems you have quit coming down to the physical world. What is going on?"

"What is going on?" the babies repeated. "What is going on down there?"

One baby spoke up in a clear voice. "Ma'am, we are very afraid of going down there these days."

"It appears to be a horrible place," another baby said, "The air and the water are polluted, and people are lying and killing one another. So many people work long, hard hours just to get by ..."

"What is the point of going there?" yet another baby screamed. "We are intelligent beings. We don't want to participate in such silly dramas."

The sage thought for a while and said, "Yes, indeed, our world has deteriorated much. You may experience a lot of pain and troubles when you are born."

"But," she continued, "you can change how things work there. Maybe you can find ways that let everyone lead a happy, fulfilling life. Maybe you can clean up the Earth. And you sure don't need to lie and kill one another."

The babies discussed this. They knew they were smart and capable, so this suggestion made sense. They even got excited anticipating the changes they would initiate.

But they had other concerns.

"While we are here, we know we are One. We love one another," said one baby. "It seems once we move to the world down there, we forget this love. Isn't that why you people lie and hurt each other?"

The sage thought for a while and said, "Yes, indeed, you will forget Oneness when you are born into individual bodies. You will likely feel lonely, at least for some time."

"But," she continued, "you can form loving relationships there. You do that by remembering the love you already know now. And when you do form relationships there, while you are in individual bodies, it adds a new dimension to the love."

The babies discussed this. They knew they were love, so eventually remembering the love didn't sound so difficult, even in a savage world. And they became curious about how love might feel when they had individualities.

After the long discussion, one baby spoke up.

"Okay, maybe going down there and being born isn't that bad after all. We have the courage to endure the temporary pain and challenges. We have the diligence to work through problems. We have the patience to wait for the time when we rediscover love."

"But is it worth it?" the baby continued. "We already love one another deeply. We already know we are One. We are happy here. There is no lack, no poverty, no hunger, no fear, no hate, no dishonesty ... This is the perfect world. Why would we want to leave here and dare to be born?"

The sage replied, "I cannot answer that question. You must find the answer for yourself. And you can find it out only when you do dare to be born."

All the babies became quiet.

And, one by one, they jumped into the twilight to be born.

SURFING THROUGH LIFE

Those who flow as life flows
know they need no other force.
— Lao Tzu

Perceptual illusions

We have started this giant simulation game of reality, and further, each of us as a soul made a life plan prior to this lifetime. Then we put a veil on ourselves to forget most of this because, if we remembered it all, there would be no fun in playing the game. By remembering only a handful of clues, we can face life spontaneously with enthusiasm and amazement.

How, then, shall we maneuver through this virtual reality game for the best effect, that is, for the highest experience of love, wisdom, and empowerment? How can we remember our Oneness while in the individual incarnation? And why are so many people living in fear and disappointment rather than in enthusiasm and amazement?

The challenge is that our perception of this world is usually faulty. For one, we see people and things instead of energy changing forms. This means we tend to ignore the ever-flowing nature of energy. However, science has found that, on the atomic level, everything is always moving. Nothing is static, even if it may appear to be standing still. Further, it is not just on the micro level. Rocks form and eventually disintegrate. The land beneath our feet is moving across the ocean. We just don't notice because our attention span is short. Many of us even see our life in stagnation, assuming today is like yesterday and tomorrow will be like today. The truth is that everything is made of energy and energy is always flowing.

Another perceptual illusion is to consider that events happen to us regardless of our thinking. We fail to notice the invisible connectedness of things and our own power to move through this virtual reality intentionally. This is the area science is still working to figure out, but there are some studies that report the significance the observer plays in experiments, such as the Schrödinger's Cat experiment. The truth is that each of us is part of the big energy flow, and we are always affecting one another and the whole energetically.

If you believe in the perceptual illusion of the static quality of this world, you might feel stuck and think you need to force your way to bring changes. You might fear that things would stay as they are if left alone. If you see the changing quality of this world but fail to notice the relevance you yourself play, even in seemingly remote events, you might fall into a victim mentality. The world might look like a crazy and scary place, over which you have little control. You might resent changes and be tempted to resist changes. You might have knee-jerk reactions to changes, which may look like bravery sometimes, but are far from it really.

Strange enough, most people have both kinds of perceptual illusions and adopt their responses quite arbitrarily. Both pushing your way for changes and resisting changes are futile ways of utilizing your energy. I call this the Fist approach to life. There is another approach to life, which I call the Flow approach.

Fist vs. Flow approach to life

At first glance, the Fist approach sounds heroic. "Go, go, go. If at first you don't succeed, try again, and never, ever, quit!" If people took such motivational talk literally, many would die from exhaustion. At the very least, it deprives us of the delight of life by always forcing us to move forward rather than cherishing what is already around us. In the Fist approach, good things must be gained and earned.

In contrast, the Flow approach accepts the flowing nature of energy and finds joy in the very changes. It is a way of nonresistance, or surrendering. It doesn't mean we powerlessly get swept away. You can still steer your boat in the direction you intend to go. Or think of it as surfing. The waves are already set, and because we have forgotten how they are programmed, they may surprise us. Still, we can ride the waves and have fun at it. This is what "problems are opportunities" means. We quit doing what doesn't work and continue to do what we choose to do, not because of some rigid dogma but because we like the feeling of the surf.

The Flow approach may seem scary, or even silly, to the ego because the ego doesn't see the energetic connectedness of all things. The benefit, however, far outweighs. We actually experience Oneness, rather than thinking about Oneness. We experience our inner divinity as we rise with the waves. It feels as if we created the waves to feel it—and in the big scheme of things, we sure did. With the Flow approach, life makes sense. So our way of life becomes simple. We don't need various rules and mottos—we just relax, feel the flow, and play with the waves.

The Flow approach is not about conforming to the popular opinion or about avoiding challenges. Conformity often means you bend yourself, and avoidance is just a form of resistance. The Flow approach starts with acceptance of who you are and how things are, and moving along the energy flow while looking to move in a certain direction. You don't force your way in that direction, but you steer with the flow. Change is easy, and even pleasant, when we live this way.

Two types of difficulties

There are, therefore, two types of difficulties in life. One is when you resist the natural flow of life. The majority of difficulties are this type and there is only one solution: surrendering. It may feel frightening, and things may get even messier than they are now, but if you don't drop your resistance, you may have to resist for the rest of your life—or until you are so exhausted that surrendering becomes almost imperative.

The other type is when you are doing everything right— that is, you are surfing well—and life suddenly presents a challenge, an unusually big wave. This is actually an honor. You are challenged because you have the power to surf through it, or more accurately, because challenge is the opportunity to remember and exercise our inner power. Just dive in and take care of things one by one, and soon you will find yourself in a wonderful place you may not have even dreamed of.

It is important to understand that there is no trick to dealing with the first type of difficulty other than dropping our resistance. Tricks only cover up the situation. You might feel better temporarily, but nothing really gets resolved and the difficulty will return soon enough. In the old days, such tricks were called black magic. In the modern day, there are various tactics and strategies that bring about the same effect. (There is what we might call good magic, which is designed to promote release. This can indeed work to the extent that the person is aware and willing to release their energetic resistance. Discussing such energetic clearing in detail is out of the scope of this book, however. Plus, we don't need such magic—plain surrendering works just fine.)

How do we know if the difficulty we are currently facing is the first type or the second? One way is to imagine what your life would be like if you surrender. For example, you might lose your relationship partner if you surrender, acknowledging you two are not getting along, and quitting compromising yourself to please him or her. Then, because you quit undermining yourself, you find yourself. If the difficulty is the result of the Fist approach to life, surrendering eventually leads to an ever-deeper realization of yourself. If you are honest with yourself—and this may take some practice because most of us are used to ignoring our own deep feelings—you will sense relief.

If, on the other hand, surrendering leads to boredom in the status quo, that means the difficulty at hand is the kind that comes along when you are in the Flow approach to life. In this case, going for the challenge leads to a greater realization of yourself. While it appears to be a difficulty, deep inside you might sense excitement, and even guidance.

As you practice the Flow approach to life, you will experience fewer and fewer of the first type of difficulties and also develop the sensitivity to know why a certain difficulty is happening in your life. It is a myth that those flowing, or surfing, through life experience no difficulties, and therefore, if you are experiencing any kind of difficulties in life, you are doing something wrong. It's just that, when you are living in the flow, difficulties cease to feel like difficulties.

How the Law of Attraction really works

The Law of Attraction is a grossly misunderstood idea. It's not really about "attracting," which sounds as if something exists outside yourself and you attract it, or pull it into your life. All the possibilities already exist in the life simulation, and you only choose one of them to manifest. The word "law" can be misleading, too. Although it works universally, we cannot prove it with our current scientific approach, so it may be more appropriate to call it a principle.

The Law of Attraction is the principle of creation. As we have been discussing, this reality is like a simulation game you play on the computer. You are presented with multiple choices over and over, and your choices create your life. How do you choose from the many options? Do you choose what appears to be a good choice? Do you choose what others seem to be choosing? Or do you avoid making conscious choices and opt for the default choice—which is a type of choice anyway. Or is there any effective way to choose?

Choose with your goal in mind, feeling as if the goal is already achieved. A popular choice or seemingly correct choice is not necessarily the choice that leads you to the experience you are seeking. When you choose thinking and feeling you are already experiencing it, you find the path to make it happen. Because time doesn't really exist, your futures already exist, and it's only a matter of choosing one future over the others. If you can feel it, it exists as possibility. Feeling guides you to make the decisions that will get you there.

It is critical that you choose consistently. For this reason, the Law of Attraction, or the principle of creation, doesn't work well when the ego uses it. As we have seen, the ego is like a small child. Can a five-year-old make consistent choices? Using the Law of Attraction from the place of the ego means you must train your ego, which is not impossible but very hard. Most people identify with the ego, and this is why the Law of Attraction hasn't worked well for them.

A more powerful way to utilize the Law of Attraction is to first disidentify with the ego and use it to experience what you, as a soul, incarnated to experience. The soul wants only one thing, to experience love. This hasn't changed since the universe started, so it's very consistent. Therefore, use the Law of Attraction to have opportunities to extend love and to deepen love. In other words, use this principle of creation to have opportunities to give.

This doesn't mean it is wrong to desire material things. For example, if providing a reasonably large and comfortable house to your family is your way of extending love, it will happen, as long as you don't negate your choice of love with your ego's fear too often. If, on the other hand, you just want a big house to show off, it will be hard, although it is still possible if you work hard to discipline your ego.

The Law of Attraction works because we are all connected. We are like parts of one body. When you intend to nourish your body with food, do you not find food and does your mouth not water? Of course, things line up for that intention. Similarly, when you intend to experience love, people and things line up—even people you have not met in this lifetime. Synchronicities happen to complete your soul's purpose. Considering that we usually identify with the ego, we can also say that synchronicity happens when we align with the flow of the universe rather than insisting the universe flow our way. And your experience of love further moves you toward even greater love. Practicing the Law of Attraction is essential in the Flow approach to life.

Training to see possibilities

An essential skill in the Flow approach to life and the practice of the Law of Attraction is to see possibilities, to see not only how things are but how they can be. Energy is always changing and it is indispensable to "read the waves," that is, to be able to imagine how things can change. Without this skill, the Flow approach quickly degrades to living passively while waiting for the next waves.

You cannot choose the option you do not see. However, choices don't always present themselves in the proverbial Y-shaped crossroads or a point in a computer game where you must make a choice to continue. Life choices are more like side roads. You are almost always moving along, so it is very easy to miss such turns and to continue to follow the path you are currently on, which means you choose by default. You need to slow down by getting into a meditative state and to develop your mental vision to see inconspicuous possibilities.

It is possible to train this ability to see possibilities, but it takes willingness. Dare to have visions. Brainstorm how things can change. You don't need to know how to bring about the changes—those are the second and third steps. For the first step, just entertain all possibilities, including what your ego criticizes as ridiculous. Many mythological stories and fairy tales are designed for this very purpose, to cultivate imagination.

From the soul's perspective, imagination means remembering the possibilities we ourselves have set prior to birth. The visions that do not really belong to you do not occur to you, and even when you somehow adopt such a vision, perhaps by reading motivational stories, it just feels foreign to you. In other words, if you can vividly imagine something happening, it is possible to happen.

Seeing possibilities is completely different from wishful thinking. For example, if you are familiar with gardening, you would envision a rich harvest of ripe tomatoes when you see the tomato seedlings in spring. If you are good at imagination, you can even visualize the grown tomato plants in your own garden. You don't see possibilities of harvesting melons, no matter how hard you try—that is the equivalent of wishful thinking.

Seeing possibilities is also different from having rigid expectations. An example of expectation in this case is to harvest a certain amount of tomatoes. Some people even have expectations of exactly how the weather should be and how the plant should grow. This is like dictating the universe to work your way—your ego's way. Things just don't flow that way, and therefore, expectation leads to resistance to how things actually are, causing the kind of difficulties that resistance causes.

Seeing a possibility does not guarantee the materialization of the possibility. It may turn out to be a cold summer and your tomato plants may not grow well. It is, nonetheless, the first step of moving toward the intended experience. If you don't see the possibility of grown tomatoes, you won't plant them in your garden.

The vision of our physical eyes can be quite deceiving. Can you visualize a beautiful butterfly when you see a caterpillar? By the same token, can you visualize future doctors, business owners, artists, or mothers and fathers, when you see little children? If not, it's time to start practicing.

The value of defiance

Most of us are used to seeing how things are and reacting to them, so training to see how things can be despite how things are now takes practice and what we might call defiance. Defiance, in this context, is not about denial or resistance. We do see and acknowledge the reality, but we don't stop there. We also acknowledge the energy is always flowing, and we hold the vision of our destination even while we are not there yet. In other words, defiance is the ability to embrace our vision as much as the reality.

One misunderstanding regarding visions is that we must know how to materialize the visions in order to justifiably have them. However, when you are in the flow, you don't need to know all the steps to get where you are heading. All you need is to steer in the direction you intend to go and be attentive and flexible to adjust the course. As we discussed in Chapter V, intuitive guidance comes step-by-step as we make progress. Not knowing all the steps up front is no excuse to disregard our great vision.

The difference between having a vision and being defiant about it versus having an expectation and insisting on it is that the first is based on our soul's intention whereas the latter is based on our ego's wishfulness. You can feel the difference. Just as an intuitive yes is a simple, clear "Yes," and the ego's insistence is lengthy and often screaming "Yes, yes, yes ... I want it ... please, please, please," vision is simple and clear whereas expectation comes with a strange loudness and is often all over the place.

Do not settle for the vision of what seems easy to materialize. If someone tells you your vision or dream is too much, just have mercy on them for their limited imagination, and be true to your own vision. If the vision is in alignment with who you are, it can happen. The change can be almost as dramatic as changing the TV station. This reality is like a simulation game, and one choice can bring out a fresh new scene. If you need assurance, read the real-life stories of people who have done something marvelous, such as Thomas Edison or Florence Nightingale, just to name a few.

Effective affirmations

Affirmation is often discussed as a way to practice the Law of Attraction. However, once you choose, you don't need to make the same choice over and over again. Repeating an affirmation has a point only as a way to condition your subconscious, not as a direct method to bring about desired changes.

Our subconscious is often confused with various contradictory ideas. When we say affirmations, ideas that do not match with the affirmations surface in our mind, and we have the chance to examine and let go of those that do not serve us. Thus, good affirmations can clarify such contradictions and help us to be consistent in the way we think, feel, and interact with the world. Once the subconscious and conscious line up in love, effective creation is only a natural result.

For your subconscious, you are always the main actor, so effective affirmations need to be in first-person voice. When the subject of an affirmation is someone else, the subconscious automatically changes it to "I." Moreover, the subconscious knows only the now, the present. It doesn't understand the past and the future very well. So effective affirmations need to be in the present tense. When affirmations are in the future tense, the subconscious gets confused and tends to stall. And the subconscious doesn't understand negation such as "not" or "no." When there are words such as "not" or "no" in the affirmation, the subconscious gets confused—it tries to skip the word, but then, the sentence without the "not" usually doesn't make sense or it contradicts your feelings.

So, in forming your affirmations, focus on what is rather than what is not. And even when the current situation doesn't match the affirmation yet, be defiant and use the present tense with confidence. Be sure it is about yourself, not someone else. For example, "I won't let anyone put me down" is an ineffective affirmation, and it might even backfire. The subconscious mind doesn't understand "won't," so this is the same as saying, "I let anyone put me down." Rather, you might want to affirm "I know my worth. I love myself." (The idea of something or someone being worthy or deserving is already a judgment call, but at least this is a good transition from the previous example.) "I will be successful and rich" is another example of an ineffective affirmation. The subconscious doesn't understand "will" and wonders when it is about—is it about now or not? Hmm ... maybe not now. Rather, see through the perceptive illusion and understand that you are already successful—it's just your current success may be a bit hard to notice yet. So instead you might want to say something like, "I am successful and enjoying my success and abundance."

Pay attention to how you feel when you say the affirmation. If you feel you are lying or faking, or if you feel even slightly uncomfortable, check your underlying beliefs. For example, suppose you are single and looking for a loving partner, so you say the affirmation, "I am happy to be with my boyfriend (or girlfriend). I am loved." By itself, this is a good affirmation. But let's say you somehow feel uncomfortable saying this. The more you say it, the more the discomfort grows in you. If something like this happens, dare to look within. In this example, check to see if you really want to hook up. Or is there something else you truly want to do, but you decided it's time for you to settle down—or at least be in a relationship? Or are there other reasons you feel uncomfortable with the prospect of an intimate relationship?

If you don't really want it, the affirmation doesn't work—and it's good that it doesn't. In such a case, the affirmation served you to realize what you truly want in life. If, on the other hand, the discomfort is due to some ungrounded fear and apprehension, you can release them with love, and once you do, you'll feel good saying the affirmation.

Find the affirmation that sounds natural to yourself and get to the place of mind that is clear of any contradiction about it. If a smile comes effortlessly to you when you say the affirmation, you are in this golden spot of alignment. Keep saying the affirmation just as long as you like.

Additionally, gratitude is a powerful affirmation. Gratitude is always in first person, present tense, and we usually focus on the positive, desirable aspect when we say words of gratitude. It acknowledges our blessings, and we can be grateful for the upcoming gifts that are on the way as well as what already has arrived.

The power of words

In a broad sense, everything we think and say works as an affirmation. We are always telling our subconscious what we think we are. So it is important not to confuse the subconscious with contradictory or counterproductive messages. Just as driving with your parking brake engaged is not a good idea, living with contradictions slows you down and causes unnecessary troubles.

Keep in mind the subconscious tends to hear your words in the first person, present tense. For example, when you say, "My boss is so mean," your subconscious interprets it to "I am so mean." And in a sense, the subconscious is right. As the saying goes, it takes one to know one. It is quite mean to focus on someone's shortcomings, and your distress matches the statement. By the same token, when you say, "She is so kind," you are telling your subconscious how kind you yourself are. Whatever we say about someone, our subconscious thinks it is about ourselves, and in a sense, it is right because we see our own reflections on others. So we might want to see others in the loving light, which means we see ourselves in the same loving light.

When you talk about, for example, how badly your ex treated you and how upset you were about it, for the subconscious, it is not about the past. The subconscious thinks something is wrong right now and notes how upset you are now—and again, in a sense, it is right. You probably are upset now and that is why you are still talking about it. When we talk about the past, we relive it, and we fail to live in the present fully. It's a good idea to be fully present and talk about the now, leaving the past in the past except when reviewing the past is necessary.

Negation works in a strange way. When you say, "I don't like this wet weather," your subconscious tries to understand it by skipping the "don't" and translates it to "I like this wet weather." But this statement doesn't match with your feeling. So the subconscious is left confused. If you tend to make many negative statements like this, you might want to practice shifting your focus from what is not to what is. For example, rather than focusing on what you don't like, focus on what you do like, and say something like, "I hope it clears up soon." Similarly, rather than saying, "I cannot do this," why not say, "I'd like to learn how to do this."

It's not about avoiding saying things that aren't nice. Unspoken affirmations are still affirmations. What we might want to do is to observe our thoughts and words as we do in meditation, and when we notice a statement that is not in alignment with who we are as souls, we might want to examine what may be causing such misunderstanding.

Letting go is easy

We cannot be in the current flow of life when we hold on to our expectations or our memory of how things were in the past. And contrary to common belief, letting go is easy.

There is nothing noble or self-sacrificing about letting go; it only restores us to sanity. If we define insanity as failing to recognize reality as it is, holding on to expectations and rejecting what is going on is a form of insanity. Similarly, holding on to the past—whether they are painful experiences or past fame—and their accompanying emotions when the reality has already changed is a form of insanity. Letting go simply restores us to sanity, enabling us to live fully now.

In other words, letting go means letting go of the delusion that we can keep things as they were or manipulate things to fit our expectations. The term implies that, if you just release your grip, it will naturally go away. You don't need to force it to go or learn various tactics to get rid of it. All you do is realize how crazy it is to live in the fantasy land of your mind at the expense of missing real opportunities in reality. After that realization, there may be a period of changing the mental habit, but that shouldn't be any more difficult than changing the habit of checking the weather on the computer instead of on TV.

What is difficult is the decision to release your hold, or to leave the fantasy land. As long as you believe that holding on to the past, for instance, gives you some advantage, you won't do it—even when it hurts so much. Many people have played the mind game so long that they are living in their mind, not reality. In their mind, they can change past events to their liking, they can punish those they think have wronged them, they can persuade others to see their point ... they can be a superstar. Holding on to expectations work in a similar way. Leaving all that and choosing the simple sanity can be daunting.

A closely related but separate issue is grief. When we lose something or someone we have loved dearly, it is natural to grieve and grieving actually promotes healing. We are doing ourselves a great favor when we take sufficient time to grieve, and trying to just "let it go" doesn't work because it's in effect an avoidance of grieving. We cannot hold on to the thing we have already lost—it is gone—but we can take time for grieving for our own recovery. When you grieve properly, there comes a time when you realize you are alive in the now, despite your loss. That's when you naturally let go of your residual grief that you don't need any longer.

Letting go of expectations includes letting go of the qualities that are not authentic to yourself. They don't belong to you, and it's a myth that you can be happy and successful by pretending to be someone else. Just like letting go of expectations, this letting go is as simple as releasing your hold, in this case your hold on to your pretense.

Letting go, however, is not about avoiding actions that you can take now. Do not use the phrase "letting go" as an excuse. When in question, ask yourself if letting it go helps you to live ever more fully now.

Let go of everything that your ego is holding on to. This is ultimately about disidentifying with the ego. Let go with love. Just as you don't need to hate the ego, letting go doesn't mean you dump with disgust.

Forgiveness, letting go, and quitting the blame game are all related, and therefore, one can lead to another. When you love who you are completely, you realize there is no one to blame, nothing to forgive, and you let go of your emotional baggage of non-love. Your sense of fault and error is replaced with the sense of peace and contentment. As you let go of what has been making the world and your life appear defective and deformed, you get to see them clearly as they are. This empowers you to create your life more freely.

When we incarnate, all we assume, as souls, is our vehicle, the body. Babies don't hold on to anything. They live today, they smile, they cry, they learn new skills, they grow, but holding on to any possessions or ideas ... that only comes much later. Blessed are those who live with the fresh attitude of a baby.

The story of an angel-in-training visiting nursing homes

Here is a mini story that shows you how expectation can drain your energy and how things can open up when you let go and live in the present reality.

An angel-in-training, disguised as a frail old woman, was visiting nursing homes.

The first one had a nice building with all the modern amenities. The meals were delicious and nutritious. It had medical staff on call 24/7. It even had a grand piano in the hall.

Nobody was in the community hall, however. The residents spent their days in their rooms, waiting for their families to visit them. When the angle-in-training knocked on their doors to say hello, they looked uninterested. They were looking into midair, dreaming of the old days when they lived with their families.

She visited several other nursing homes. Some were in a beautiful countryside, some had park-like yards and well-equipped sports facilities, but the residents looked the same: uninterested and absentminded. Almost lifeless. The angel-in-training felt so sorry for them but didn't know what to do. During her training, she learned that forcing people to do things, even good things such as visiting their aging parents at nursing homes, wasn't a good idea.

Although she was very discouraged, she dragged her feet to yet another nursing home. This was a mediocre-looking apartment-like building. When she walked up to the door, however, she heard laughter! Maybe, she thought, this is where the residents' families cared enough to visit often.

When she entered, however, she saw only old people. It was they who were laughing happily like kids. The angel-in-training couldn't help asking why they were so happy.

"Oh, this nursing home has twenty-four residents. Twenty-four friends who live close by and get to do things together!" an old woman responded.

"But ... does your family visit you?" asked the angel-in-training.

To this, she answered, "Sometimes."

Another resident said, "Not really."

Yet another mumbled, "I don't have a family."

And this was when the angel-in-training understood that love and joy are always within arm's reach.

Applying the understanding to your life

We have reviewed how our reality started with the split of the primordial energy. Each of us is an extension of the Source, and as such, exists on two levels, in the greater reality and the so-called reality, as spirit and as individualized soul. We have looked into the difference between the ego and the soul, and how we can disidentify with the ego. We saw our life as a soul that goes beyond physical birth and death. Then we reviewed the three aspects of the Source energy: love, wisdom, and power. All three are ultimately about our Oneness. Finally, we examined how we can live in accordance with the energy flow.

Now, the big question is: how can we apply our understanding to real life? Perhaps you are facing major life challenges such as divorce or serious health issues. Or maybe your loved one is. There are so many questions: Is it better to stay together or is divorce preferable? Preferable to whom? What if there are children involved? What if alcoholism and other substance abuse is the main concern—should you give your partner a second chance if they are willing to go to rehab? How can you trust them? What if violence is involved? What if you live in a society in which divorce puts you at a serious social and financial disadvantage? These are just a few typical concerns with divorce, and divorce is just one challenge in life.

There are no solutions that work for all seemingly similar cases because every single case is different. Therefore, you are the only person who can make the best decision about your life. It would be disrespectful of me or anyone to tell you what to do or to criticize your decisions. And this is why we have discussed in length self-love, intuition development, and empowerment. I hope you realize that you have the full wisdom and power, along with supporting love, to make the best decision for yourself.

Bewilderment in the flow

The life simulation presents challenges whether we live with the Flow approach or the Fist approach. It's just that, with the Fist approach, you can pretend you have controlled order, while with the Flow approach, the challenge is messy, and you might feel you don't even know who you are anymore. This isn't bad, however. It's a process of disidentifying with the ego, and therefore, it takes you to the realization of Oneness. Be open and vulnerable, allow yourself to feel all emotions, and keep surfing in life.

Energy is always flowing, and like the change of seasons, it is not always orderly. Sometimes things appear to be going back and forth. Sometimes we are hit with storms. A storm doesn't mean you are abandoned. Rather, it means you are entrusted to live through it. It's not about holding your breath while you wait for the storm to pass. One of the most counter-productive pieces of advice is "It's going to be okay. The best is yet to come." While this advice is intended to encourage those who are going through tough times, it only shifts our atten-tion from the present to the future. Thus, it closes our mind to the blessings that are present in the storm.

On the deeper level, it is not some external force that is bringing the storms. We have planned them. Chaos is often discussed negatively; for those in the Fist approach to life, chaos is what happens when they fail to micromanage. However, when you live with the Flow approach to life that embraces our innate creative power, you find a new meaning for chaos. Creativity isn't sterile. A truly creative artist's studio is lively and messy; that's how they experiment and find new combinations. As the creator of our own life, we want to value creative chaos, rather than obsessively keep order. What someone in the Fist approach might fear or condemn as chaotic is the birthplace of new possibilities.

In other words, we don't always have to have a plan. We can relax. When things happen, live them. When they end, move on. Accept and enjoy bewilderment in the flow. Abandon your ego's small smartness and open up to the unknown wisdom. Quit defining yourself and float in boundless love.

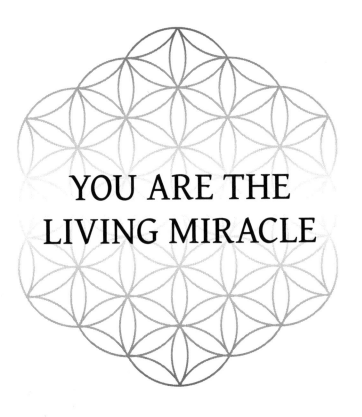

YOU ARE THE
LIVING MIRACLE

*There are only two ways to live your life.
One is as though nothing is a miracle.
The other is as though
everything is a miracle.*
— Albert Einstein

Accepting our Oneness

In Chapter I, I wrote that our purpose is "to realize Oneness while still taking the individualized forms; to experience our innate love in the world of phenomena where non-love feels real." Our purpose is not Oneness but to realize Oneness. Oneness itself is not something to be achieved. We are One as spirit already.

What we are working on is to remember and accept this Oneness. While we often think Oneness or love is something we choose, the truth, seen from the greater reality, is that Oneness is all there is and it is we that have been created so that Oneness can experience itself. This doesn't mean we are powerless pawns—we are the Oneness, the one life that has become the souls, temporarily incarnating in this world of phenomena.

Some people call this realization of Oneness enlightenment, and if so, enlightenment is available to everyone, anytime. It takes only a shift of attention, from this reality to the greater reality, from our false identification with the ego to our true self, the soul.

It is critical to understand that Oneness is not a goal. When we think of oneness as a goal, we strive for it and force it onto others. Then oneness becomes a form of totalitarian control, perhaps with a spiritual flavor. People who think this way might say something like, "You shouldn't be acting selfish like that. We are one." In this false oneness, diversity and individual independence are undermined, and fear, not love, becomes the rule because people are judged by how well they live up to the standard of unity. Confusion is also inevitable because nobody can be sure exactly what that standard may be. Needless to say, this is not what we aspire to.

Oneness is not about communism and abandonment of personal possessions, either. If someone doesn't like the idea of personal possessions, they are free to donate everything they have. Doing so might help them feel free and, as a form of service, might help them disidentify with the ego. They still need to respect others' lifestyles, however. Realization of Oneness comes through our free will. It cannot be forced onto others or onto oneself because the moment it is forced, it becomes a false oneness.

Diversity is essential in true Oneness because it is through the unique individual perspectives that we experience life and see the whole. All the various perspectives are valuable for one reason or another. An extreme example is Hitler. Because Hitler has already shown us that ethnic discrimination and mass killing, along with underlying hate, doesn't work, we don't have to do that again. Again, Hitler is an extreme example, but most of us have some people against whom we carry some grudge, and realizing Oneness means forgiving them and acknowledging their roles in Oneness. This is why Jesus demonstrated forgiveness for tax collectors, prostitutes, and those who persecuted him.

Accepting Oneness means accepting that everyone, including those whose choices may feel wrong to you, is part of the Oneness. Oneness is not conditional. This means you don't have to do anything to earn your place in Oneness. You are included in the universal Oneness already. This is the great news, the most wonderful blessing.

Everyone is my extended self

Because we are all made of the same Source energy, we can say there is only one being in the whole universe. This one being is taking the form of me, of you, of everyone and everything. In this perspective, everyone is my extended self, and I am the extended self of everyone.

When we recognize the traits in others that we ourselves acknowledge to possess and value, we like those people. This is how friendships and relationships start. Quite similarly, when we recognize the traits in others that we ourselves know we possess but try to deny, we tend to dislike those people. We have been trying so hard to fix those traits or hide them in ourselves—how dare they shamelessly present the same? It isn't really about them or their character defects. It's about ourselves, our traits, and how we feel about them.

We project our feelings onto others. Relationship problems are not about the relationship but about two individuals projecting their own problems onto each other. While our awareness is unclear, it is easier to project and observe our reflection on others than to look into oneself. The partner serves as the mirror, and the problems dissolve when the projector realizes the issues within that have long been suppressed. Everyone is everyone else's mirror in one way or another.

When someone upsets me and therefore prompts me to heal the part of me that is reacting, that someone is unknowingly doing a favor for me. My extended self, in the form of that person, came around and pointed out my old wound that I myself have forgotten. And because we are all One, I heal you and the world when I heal myself.

Likewise, when someone causes me a problem, that someone is creating an opportunity for me to exercise my power. My extended self, in the form of that person, crossed my path and reminded me of my inner wisdom and power. When I use the problem as an opportunity to move to the direction I intend to go, I influence not only my life but also the whole universe.

You have been that person for me, and I have been one for you. Everyone, including those I have not met in this lifetime, is my extended self. There is only one being in the whole universe. There is only the universal energy.

And this is why individuality is critical. If the one energy were to manifest into all the same pieces, there would be no point in manifesting and playing this virtual reality game. By the way you are different from me, you show me who I am—far bigger and more complex than I thought I was. You are my guiding light. And because I can see your light, I know my light within. The light within is ultimately the same as the light I see without. Self-love and love for others are the same, and choosing one over the other is ultimately impossible.

Connection to all beings

Further, it is not only the people but also all animals, plants, minerals, and things that are my extended self. We are all connected energetically. It is not so hard to feel this connection. Simply take some quiet time looking up at the stars or walking in the woods. In a sense, it is rather ridiculous to think humans are separated from the rest of the universe and that each person, animal, plant, and thing is cut off from the rest.

Or you can use some imagination to stimulate your awareness. For example, look at a tree and imagine how you may appear from the tree's perspective. As you contemplate this and silently enter the meditative state, you will know. We can even say that the very reason you are here in the human form now is to complete your awareness as a tree—if we think in terms of linear time. You were a tree, and now you are seeing a tree; thus, you are now aware how a tree is when seen from a human eye. Likewise, the tree is completing your awareness of yourself.

Dream

I saw birds.
That night, I dreamed I was a bird.
I flew freely and chirped in joy. I trusted my wings to take me to the height I didn't yet know.

I saw flowers.

That night, I dreamed I was a flower.

I marveled at my own beauty. I was comfortable knowing the butterflies were coming to me.

I saw mountains.

That night, I dreamed I was a mountain.

I was big and stable. I embraced trees and animals in the storm.

I woke up and remembered I was all of them, and more.

I still had the confidence of the bird, the love of the flower, and the generosity of the mountain.

Since then, I keep seeing myself in everything and everything in myself.

Everything happens for us

When we understand there is only one being in the greater reality, we understand that, despite how it may appear, everything happens for us. Everything is either a straightforward blessing or a disguised blessing. All lead us to the experience of love, if we so choose.

For example, imagine someone who has been married for many years. Then he or she finds that their spouse has been cheating. This is a heavily emotional experience. They might feel devastated. How can this experience lead to greater love? It looks like they lost the love of their life.

But really? If the spouse has been cheating and lying, this spouse's love is not what their partner thought it was, and even when the partner was unaware of the affair, they probably sensed the change. The romantic love ended long ago, and the couple has only been keeping the facade of what used to be love. The disclosure of the spouse's affair can serve as the push for them to stand up for themselves and thereby nurture their self-love. Further, in their new single life, they might find the blessings of friendship. If they keep their heart open, they will realize that, even with that experience, life goes on, and they are loved and protected by something far bigger than words can describe.

This person didn't lose love. The specific form of love ended long ago. They can use this occasion as the jump board to realize greater love—if they so choose. It's also possible to live the rest of their life in bitter resentment against their spouse and life in general.

Another example. Think of someone who suddenly loses their job through no fault of their own. In addition to financial difficulties, they might feel betrayed by the company for which they have been working hard for many years. They might feel a part of their identity is lost. How can this experience be a disguised blessing?

There are various cases, but for instance, this person may have been thinking of starting their own business but couldn't leave the seeming security of the corporate job. Because they were let go, they have the opportunity to test their idea, which is a way to honor oneself. This doesn't necessarily mean their business will succeed—no business is easy, and small business is especially challenging. However, the blessing is in the challenge itself. They get to know themselves and the world in a whole new way that wasn't possible as a corporate employee.

We don't always understand how a given situation leads to greater wisdom, power, and love. Sometimes, we just have to trust life. It is wonderful that the wisdom of the Source is not limited by our current understanding of things. Because some people choose to call the Source God, this trust in life is also faith. This is why we say God always loves us whether we understand it or not.

This is not the so-called positive thinking. Positive thinking is great if it is about accepting everything and seeing the positive value in all, despite how things may appear. In recent years, however, false positive thinking that teaches people to focus on the positive—or what they judge to be positive—has become popular. Such false positive thinking is based on judgment and advocates ignoring what appears to be negative or unfavorable. Just as ignoring and suppressing the so-called negative emotions effectively keep them strong under the surface, ignoring what you fear to be negative doesn't resolve them. It only leads you to more and more judgments and fear based on such judgments. Life gets constrained with such false positive thinking. In contrast, what we might call true positive thinking acknowledges everything and understands life is wonderful even with challenges—or because of the challenges.

When we realize that everything happens for us, we naturally drop our resistance and live in the flow of life. We see that we don't need to control our lives—we can relax. Waves come, and we ride them with joy and excitement. Some waves are huge and we might fall. That's okay. We will recover, and next time we have a better chance to ride big waves. We also enjoy the calm water, catching our breath and enjoying the view. Acceptance, gratitude, and love fill our heart no matter what happens in our life.

Our Earth walk

We are the Oneness creating the reality to experience itself. Challenges are never bad—we create them to make the game more interesting. In other words, life cannot be against us because we are the one creating it. It's only our ego that finds certain situations problematic.

Let's dispel the myth that life is a school and we are here to learn lessons. If life was a school where we must strive to learn lessons and take exams—and if we fail the exam, we must come back until we pass, at which point we move on to yet another lesson, another exam—life would be a dreadful hell itself. The good news is it is not. As extensions of the Source, that is perfection, we already know all the spiritual truths. We are here to experience what we already know. Therefore, spiritual growth is also a myth. We don't become better, and we don't need to beat ourselves up to be better. We only shed our ideas of a fragmented self to realize our wholeness.

Life is not about repaying karma, either. The soul knows only to love, and as souls, we don't keep karmic scores and hold someone liable. We owe nothing to anyone. Each of us keeps our own karmic records for our reference so that we can try new ways.

Life is a virtual reality simulation. We choose to incarnate because exploring the endless manifestations of love is interesting—just as playing a sophisticated game is challenging yet interesting and fun. And the marvelous thing is that we are not just players in this game but also the designers of the game.

So life is also a studio. We come to this world of phenomena to experiment and create new combinations. Creation is endless. While each piece of creative product can be wonderful in its own right, there is always more to create. For example, Picasso kept creating all his life. After creating masterpieces of cubism that made him world-famous, he moved on to explore other ways of expression—not because there was anything wrong with his early creations, but because creation is fun. Mozart was the same way. Once he wrote a piece of music, he knew even he himself could not improve it further, so he wrote another one. And another. We keep creating our lives in the same way, with inexhaustible curiosity and enthusiasm.

Our souls are not imprisoned in our bodies, and our earthly life is not a punishment. We, as souls, chose to incarnate, and everything in our lives is an endorsement of our choice. Therefore, our purpose to realize Oneness and to experience love is not achieved in some distant future. It is in each moment, in the here and now. Even when the current moment seems so humble, even mundane. Even when something that appears to be unfavorable is happening.

✳ ✳ ✳

Our Earth Walk

This is our Earth walk.
This day. This evening.
The traffic jam.
The cranky boss and customers.
Thinking about what to eat for dinner.
Hearing from a friend.
Someone dying.
Someone having a baby.
The sunset.
Taking out trash.
The moment before falling asleep.
This is our Earth walk.
This one step. And another.
The meaning is in each step.

Giving and receiving are the same

Because there is only one being, giving and receiving are ultimately the same. They are both about allowing energetic flow. When we refuse either one, we block the natural flow.

When we give, we create a space within ourselves for the new. Being stingy and energetically constipated eventually leaves us stuffed, making it difficult for the fresh, nurturing energy to come in. When we dare to give, the outflow of giving creates the inflow of receiving.

When we refuse to receive, we deprive someone of the opportunity to give. It is actually a very arrogant behavior that disrupts the natural energy flow, and eventually we become isolated. Receiving is a humbling act that acknowledges the imperfection of the individual self, and when we dare to receive, we open up to the universal Oneness.

Needless to say, giving and receiving don't need to be reciprocal. Expecting to receive something when we give or planning to give back when we receive limits the energy flow within that small circle. When we understand everyone and everything in the universe are interconnected, we can give and receive openly and freely.

So don't just be kind. Let people be kind to you. Give them the opportunity to express their love for you. And receive with grace. You don't need to give back anything—a smile and a thank-you would be nice, but even that is not a requirement. When you give, give indiscriminately without worrying if someone deserves to receive. And we can always give. It can be some money, an act of kindness (some of which are so easy to do that we hardly consider them as kindness), a friendly "Hi," … the possibilities are endless. We will find that, the more we give and share without expectation, the more we have to give.

You are deeply loved

As I complete this book, the message that comes through so clearly, so warmly, and so gracefully is that we are all deeply loved and we are okay. If there is just one thing that you take away, let it be the comfort and assurance that you are loved, and whatever you are going though, you are okay. If there is just one thing you might do because you have read this book, let it be to live each day knowing you are loved. Let that big love flow through you. This way, we live in constant love.

If you are struggling, please know you are loved. What you are experiencing is not a punishment. You didn't do anything wrong. You may not yet understand how it will work out in your life, but it will when you let it. You are deeply loved.

If you are dying, please know you are loved. Death is nothing but a transformation. Farewell is sad. I feel for your pain, and I hope the transition will be as comforting as it can be. Don't torture yourself emotionally in addition to the sadness of farewell and the physical pain you may be feeling. You are deeply loved.

Every single being is deeply loved already. You do not need to jump through hoops to qualify to be loved. Everything you have done has served the purpose. And whatever you have done, or have failed to do, you cannot not be loved. You are loved and you are love itself. We come from the loving energy of the Source. Love is who we are.

I originally wrote this poem when my friend had a grand-child, but I think it also serves as a blessing for all of us.

Beloved

There is not only one flower,
not only many flowers of one kind,
but many, many flowers of many, many kinds
filling the field for your arrival.

There is not only one voice,
not only many voices of one tone,
but many, many voices of many, many tones
singing in harmony celebrating your arrival.

So please, the beloved one, do not take this life too seriously.
The sun that grows the flowers is with you.
The conductor who orchestrates the music is with you.

The world shines when you smile
because you are also the flower and the voice.

The greatest miracle

Love is a miracle. As physical beings, it is natural to prioritize
survival and self-benefit, and love defies this—and we delight
in it. Intuition is a miracle. It utilizes the resource an individual brain is not supposed to have access to. Synchronicity

is a miracle. Why do people and things line up when we quit forcing them to work our way?

The greatest mystery and miracle, however, is life itself and that we exist on two levels, in the greater reality and the so-called reality, at the same time. This means we are already One while we appear separate, leading individual lives. This miracle makes it possible to experience the two seemingly contradictory values side by side: Oneness and individuality, unity and uniqueness. This great miracle is the foundation of all other miracles such as love, intuition, and synchronicity.

This book, then, is not about explaining life. Explanation would be an insult to you. This book is about helping you remember the sense of wonder in you. The life you are creating is indeed wonderful, and the world is filled with miracles. Please do not betray yourself by being cynical or withdrawn. The childlike sense of wonder brightens your eyes and guides you.

We all come from the Source. The infinitely intelligent Source split and became individual beings so that it can know itself. Because time doesn't really exist, the split is not just something that happened long ago—it is always happening. You are one of the holographic extensions of the Source, and therefore, you are the Source. To understand this great creation is to understand your divinity. Each of us and all life forms and things, whether they are currently incarnated and manifest or not, are such extensions of the Source. You are the living miracle.

Bibliography

Mitchell, Stephen. *Tao Te Ching*. New York: HarperCollins Publishers, 1988.

About the Author

Akemi G has been offering professional Akashic Record Reading through her website: www.akashicrecordreading.com

She is originally from Japan and has been living in the United States since 1995. She is proud of her multicultural background, which supports her ability to communicate with a wide range of people worldwide.

Her coauthors—her spirit guides who have disclosed the ideas in this book—prefer to stay anonymous. For inquiries and comments, please contact Akemi.

Made in the USA
Lexington, KY
19 January 2015